The
SWANAGE BRANCH
IN COLOUR

The Ultimate Archive

Andrew P. M. Wright

This book is dedicated to the memory of the many Swanage branch line staff over the years – and to those who rebuilt, run, develop and extend the Swanage Railway today.

Contents

Copyright Andrew P. M. Wright
& Kingfisher Productions 2013
Designed and published by Roger Hardingham
ISBN 978-0-9573367-3-5
Printed in the United Kingdom

Published by
Kingfisher Productions
Watershed Mill
Settle
North Yorkshire
BD24 9LR
www.railwayvideo.com

With the home signal showing a clear line to Corfe Castle on Thursday, 9 December, 1971, a train for Swanage climbs the main line 1 in 200 gradient from Wareham towards Worgret Junction and the start of the ten-mile single line beyond the A352 road bridge. *John A.M. Vaughan courtesy of Rail Photoprints*

A driver's view from a train bound for Corfe Castle and Swanage as it swings on to the branch at Worgret Junction with signalman Eddie Brown preparing to hand over the single line key token, in its pouch, for Corfe Castle on Thursday, 9 December, 1971. *John A.M. Vaughan courtesy of Rail Photoprints*

Acknowledgements

I would like to thank the many friends who have very kindly and generously helped with my almost 30 years of researches into the history of the Swanage branch line – Roger Aldous, Gerry Andrews, Mike Arlett, the late Hugh Ballantyne, John H. Bird, Jim Boudreau, the Bournemouth Railway Club for access to the late Roy Brough collection, Bob Bishop, Melvyn Cox, John Coleman, Colin Caddy, John Carter, John Chalcraft of Rail Photoprints, Paul Chancellor of Colour Rail, Roger Cruse, Terence Dorrity, Tim Deacon, Mike Esau, Peter Foster, Peter Frost, the late Bryan Green, Laurie Golden, John Spencer Gilks, Alan Greatbatch, Jimmy Hunt, Michael Hardy, Roy Hobbs, Richard and Shirley Hordle, Les Hayward, Danny Hathaway, Stan Hoey, the late Bob Inman, Brian Jackson, Mark Jamieson, Steve Jenkins, Tony Jervis, the late Frank Kitcatt, the late Brian Kohring, Chris Leigh, Rodney Lissenden, David Lockett, Graham Mallinson, Gavin Morrison, George Moon, Dave Mant, Mick Miller, Malcolm Munro, Andrew Naylor, the late Fred Norman, Keith Pfrangley, Chris Phillips, the late George Pryer, Bob Richards, the late R.C. Riley, Geoff Rixon, Kevin Robertson, John Rowley, Malcolm Smith, Roger Smith, Tim Stephens, Geoff Sharpe, John Scrace, Colin Stone, Peter Sills, Peter Swift, Alan Trickett, Geoff Truscott, Trevor Owen, Tony Trood, Mike Turner, Barry Thirlwall, Les Tindall, Martyn Thresh, John Vaughan, Mark Woolley, Mike Walshaw, Alan Wild, Terry Williams, Cliff Woodhead and Peter Zabek. Special thanks to my publisher Roger Hardingham at Kingfisher Productions.

Introduction

In this book, you can travel back in time and enjoy the largest collection of Swanage branch colour photographs ever assembled – from the heyday of the Purbeck line in 1951 through to its sad and controversial end in 1972.

The ten-mile Swanage line was opened in 1885 when the world's first car design was patented, the first skyscraper was built, the Statue of Liberty arrived by sea in New York, the first cafeteria and petrol pump came into use in the United States and the Mikado comic opera opened for the first time in London.

British Rail controversially closed the line in 1972 – the year of the last Apollo manned mission to the Moon, when British Prime Minister Edward Heath declared a state of emergency during the miners' strike, the *Queen Elizabeth* liner sank in Hong Kong harbour after being destroyed in a fire and the Watergate burglary in Washington took place which was to bring down American president Richard Nixon.

'The Swanage Branch in Colour – The Ultimate Archive' has been produced to mark the Swanage Railway announcement in February, 2013, that a regular community train service will be running from Swanage and Corfe Castle to the main line at Wareham during 2015, thanks to an historic £1.47 million Government grant.

After a battle of almost 40 years to build a railway from Wareham to Corfe Castle and Swanage, construction work started at Worgret – a mile west of Wareham on the London to Weymouth line – and at Swanage in May, 1883. Excluding the rails, the cost was £80,000 – £5 million in today's money – and the line opened in May, 1885; transforming Swanage from a quiet quarrying, fishing and farming community into a thriving seaside resort.

The new branch line's impact on the Isle of Purbeck was tremendous; a Victorian train journey from Wareham to Swanage taking 25 minutes and costing eleven old pence instead of the 90-minute horse and carriage trip via the villages of Kingston and Langton Matravers which cost two shillings and sixpence.

Opening up the picture postcard village of Corfe Castle to tourism, the new line also enabled stone, ball clay and livestock to be exported from the Isle of Purbeck – and coal, as well as other day-to-day items, to be brought into Corfe Castle and Swanage by rail.

The Swanage branch was not a victim of the infamous Beeching Report in March, 1963, but British Rail managers privately wanted to close the line from the summer of 1966.

It did not fit in with their plans for the London to Bournemout electrification – diesel push-pull trains running onwards to Poole, Wareham, Dorchester and Weymouth – with claims that the Swanage branch line carried less passengers and lost money.

The archetypal branch line scene fitting seamlessly into the Purbeck countryside during the year the Berlin Wall went up. Victorian-designed M7 tank No. 30379 pushes a two-coach Maunsell push-pull set into Corfe Castle station with a train from Wareham to Swanage on Wednesday, 14 June, 1961. In the 'up' platform, a Southern Railway 'Q' class steam locomotive pauses while working light engine back to Bournemouth, having brought in a goods train to Swanage and undertaken shunting duties. *Cliff Woodhead.*

The line to Corfe Castle and Swanage was not included in Labour Transport Minister Barbara Castle's 'British Railways Network for Development' map of March, 1967, and the first official closure proposal for the line was published in the Times newspaper during October, 1967. After repeated objections from local councils and the public, British Rail finally closed the Swanage branch on the morning of Monday, 3 January, 1972 – the last train running on the Saturday night because there was no winter Sunday service – and the tracks were quickly lifted during that summer.

Having first walked the abandoned undergrowth-choked trackbed from Corfe Castle to Swanage as a 15-year-old in 1980, it has been an exciting privilege to play a part – as a volunteer for more than 30 years – in the rebuilding of the branch line, against all the odds, back to the national railway network. The Swanage Railway proves that preservation really is the art of achieving the impossible!

I would like to thank the featured photographers for having the foresight, and skill, to take such wonderful colour images between 1950 and 1972 – despite colour film being expensive and having low sensitivity to light. I hope that you enjoy this book, and delight in the colour of the Swanage branch, as much as I have enjoyed its research and compilation over the years.

Andrew P.M. Wright

The end of steam and an era dating back to 1885. Running half an hour late, the last British Rail steam train from Swanage prepares to leave the station with Standard Class 4 Tank No. 80146 leading a 12-coach Railway Correspondence and Travel Society 'Farewell to Southern Steam Tour' bound for Corfe Castle and Wareham at 2.30pm on Sunday, 18 June, 1967. With Swanage signal box having been closed less than two weeks before, the signals have been stripped of their enamel arms with the track points clipped and bolted.
Andrew P.M. Wright Collection

A Journey to Swanage

A driver's eye view of the western approach to Wareham in 1966 from a Class 47 diesel-electric on the summer Sundays Swanage to Eastleigh train. With the level crossing gates open for road traffic, the train is being held at the 'up' home signal. To the left and right are the north and south bay platforms No. 1 and No. 4 arriving and departing Swanage trains with the 'Up Siding West' behind the signal. All three tracks were lifted in late 1976. To the right is the water tower demolished in 1972. *Chris Phillips*

The start of a 22-minute journey to Swanage on the morning of Monday, 27 August, 1962. LSWR Dugald Drummond M7 0-4-4 tank No. 30057 simmers in the 'down' south bay platform No. 1 at Wareham with a two-coach 'Ironclad' coach set. Behind the 1887 station building is the 1847 station master's house. *Gavin W. Morrison*

Wareham shunter/guard Jim 'Paddy' Mulqueen in the summer of 1966 as Standard Class 4 2-6-0 No. 76013 prepares to shunt its two Mark One coaches into the 'down' south bay platform No. 1 – having run round its stock in the 'up' main platform No. 3 – before departing for Swanage. To the left is the 'up' north bay platform No. 4 where Swanage trains arrived. An ordnance depot siding led off the north bay track between 1918 and 1924.
Arthur Wooller via Roger Smith

With the fireman leaning out, M7 tank No. 30057 trundles into Wareham and the 'up' north bay platform No. 4 with an 'Ironclad' push-pull coach set from Swanage on Monday, 27 August, 1962. Built at Nine Elms in 1906, No. 30057 was a branch regular and based at Bournemouth from 1956. She was withdrawn in 1963, and scrapped at Eastleigh that July. To the left is the line into the 'down' south bay platform No. 1.
Gavin W. Morrison

Above: M7 tank No. 30111 simmers with its two-coach 'Ironclad' push-pull set in the 'down' south bay platform No. 1 at Wareham ahead of its ten-mile trip to Corfe Castle and Swanage on Wednesday, 5 September, 1962. Unofficially known as 'Lord Nelson' in its younger days, and built in 1904, No. 30111 first moved to Bournemouth in 1931 – returning in 1948 before being withdrawn in January, 1964. *George M. Moon*

Left: Veteran Swanage branch driver Jack Spicer oils the motion of an Ivatt tank in the 'down' south bay platform No. 1 at Wareham during the summer of 1966 before the next departure for Corfe Castle and Swanage. A real character, Jack started his railway career at Dover in Kent before moving to the Swanage branch after the Second World War. Well known for frequently oiling his locomotive and drinking water from his enamel tea can, Jack retired in September, 1966, when steam ended on the Swanage branch and the train service was operated by 'Hampshire' diesel-electric multiple units. *Chris Phillips*

Above: The crew of Ivatt 2-6-2 tank No. 41260 – Swanage driver Jack 'Johnny' Spicer, fireman Bruce Skitteral in his white peaked cap with two chrome stars – and station shunter Bert Samson at Wareham's 'up' main platform No. 3 while running round the Swanage branch train during the summer of 1964. After the end of the M7 tanks in May, 1964, the non-push-pull fitted locomotives ran round their coaches between the main platforms using the crossovers. No. 41260 will reverse the stock into the 'down' south bay platform No.1 before departing for Swanage. Jack started on the South Eastern and Chatham Railway in the early 1920s. *Chris Phillips*

Right: The human face of British Railways. Some of Wareham's station staff in 1966 during the last full summer of main and branch line steam. From left are shunter/guard Jim 'Paddy' Mulqueen, leading porter Gordon Bessant and booking clerk Les Hurst. 'Paddy' Mulqueen retired in 1990 after joining British Railways in 1957. *Chris Phillips*

Above: Wareham signal box on Friday, 6 August, 1971, with the station platforms out of view to the left. Built opposite the site of the 1847 original station, the 1928 signal box is due to close during 2014 with the completion of the £32 million Poole to Wool re-signalling scheme. Main line trains through Wareham – and those from Corfe Castle and Swanage – will then be controlled from Basingstoke. *Mike Walshaw*

Left: The interior of Wareham signal box and its 30-lever frame designed by Stevens and built under licence by Tyer's in 1928. From left to right on the block shelf is the Wareham to Hamworthy or Poole block bell tapper; the Wareham to Wool three position block instrument; the Wareham to Wool block bell; a spare lever collar; the north bay platform No. 4 'train arrived complete' bell; a locking release; the direct line telephone to Keysworth crossing; a Bardic lamp; the 'up' sidings shunt bell; the Wareham to Hamworthy or Poole block bell; the Wareham to Hamworthy or Poole three position block instrument and finally the Wareham to Wool block bell tapper. *Bob Richards*

A goods train from Swanage and Corfe Castle bound for Poole yard, and onward to Eastleigh, pauses at Wareham's 'up' platform on the morning of Monday, 31 August, 1964, with Standard Class '4' 2-6-0 tender locomotive No. 76019 at its head. In the distance is one of two crossing keeper's cottages, demolished in early 1967, while cars stream over the level crossing and the signalman in his signal box waits to open the gates and allow the Purbeck freight train on its way. *George M. Moon*

Passengers hurry off Wareham's 'up' platform on the morning of Monday, 31 August, 1964, as Bournemouth driver of Standard Class '4' Tank No. 80147, Graham 'George' Mansbridge, 'eases up' so his fireman can uncouple the 1954 Brighton-built locomotive from its two Maunsell push-pull carriages as Wareham station foreman Jack Hood looks on. Always smart and wearing his full uniform, Jack retired from Wareham in the early 1970s. Push-pull trains to Swanage ceased with the end of the M7 tanks in May, 1964, so No. 80147 will run round its train and leave from the 'up' platform No. 3 or reverse the carriage set into the north bay platform No. 4 ahead of its next departure for Corfe Castle. *George M. Moon*

Left: The fireman of M7 tank No. 30108 'Rosie' keeps a lookout on the 'up' main line at Wareham on Saturday, 13 April, 1963, while shunting a 24-tank Kimmeridge oil train. The tanks were stored in the 'Up Siding East', next to the signal box, and filled by road tankers from the Purbeck oil field before the loaded train was hauled to an oil refinery at Ellesmere Port in Cheshire. On the side of 30108's smokebox is the push-pull Westinghouse pump and regulator control cylinder. *Alan Wild*

Above: Wareham station staff in the summer of 1967 after push-pull diesel trains replaced steam on the main line between Bournemouth and Weymouth. From left are shunter Bert Sansom, shunter/guard Jim 'Paddy' Mulqueen, booking clerk Rex Spinney and leading railman Les Masters in his new 1967 British Rail uniform. Behind is the station footbridge and the Railway Hotel. *Chris Phillips*

Left: Another view of No. 30108 'Rosie' shunting the Kimmeridge oil train at Wareham on Saturday, 13 April, 1963. Behind the train is the 'up' north bay platform No. 4. The first oil was commercially extracted from Kimmeridge in 1960. M7 No. 30108 obtained its two pink rose transfers in the zeros of its bunker number before working the Railway Enthusiasts' Club 'Rambling Rose' push-pull railtour of Hampshire, Wiltshire, Berkshire and Surrey on Saturday, 23 March, 1963. *Alan Wild*

The fascination of steam at Wareham before a departure for Corfe Castle and Swanage during early 1966. In awe of ex-LMS Ivatt tank No. 41320 as it simmers in the 'down' south bay platform No. 1 with a rake of two 1940s Bulleid coaches, the children would now be aged in their late 50s. To the right is the yard of H.V. Perry Transport. Ivatt tanks appeared on branch trains in late 1963 as the M7 tanks were dying out. *Roy Brough*

Driver Jock Habgood and fireman Ken Hordle water M7 tank No. 30052 at the end of Wareham's 'down' platform on the evening of Thursday, 29 August, 1963. Jock retired in September, 1966, while Ken drove 'Hampshire' diesel-electric multiple units to Swanage until the end in 1972. Joining British Railways in 1953 as cleaner at Bournemouth, Ken was loaned to the Swanage branch and became a main line London to Weymouth driver on Class 33 and 47 diesels, TC and REP units as well as Class 73 electro-diesels during the 1970s. *Rodney A. Lissenden*

Left: M7 tank No. 30057 propels its 'Ironclad' push-pull set out of the 'down' south bay platform No. 1 at Wareham and past the starting signal bound for Corfe Castle on Monday, 27 August, 1962. The station water tower is to the left while a Maunsell push-pull set is berthed in the 'Up Siding West' beyond the train. *Gavin W. Morrison*

Below: Away to the west as M7 tank No. 30107 propels its Maunsell push-pull set up the 1 in 200 gradient out of Wareham bound for Worgret Junction on Saturday, 27 October, 1962. The train is about to pass over the first River Piddle bridge. No more than three carriages could be propelled without a guard. No. 30107 was built at Nine Elms in 1904 before moving to Bournemouth in 1937 for 13 years. The M7 returned to Bournemouth in 1951 and was withdrawn in March, 1964. *Gavin W. Morrison*

Above: Ivatt 2-6-2 Tank No. 41316 climbs the 1 in 200 gradient to Worgret Junction past Wareham Common with three 1940s Bulleid coaches in tow on Saturday, 26 June, 1965. The junction signalman has pulled off the home signal for the branch so the train has a clear run to Corfe Castle. On the skyline to the right is the chimney of the rail-connected Victorian Sandford pottery built in 1866, closed in 1966 and demolished in 1979. *Alan Trickett*

Right: Having just run off the branch, BR Standard Class 3 2-6-2 tank no. 82028 blows off as it hauls its Maunsell set No. 609 from the 'down' to the 'up' line at Worgret Junction with the 12.30pm train from Swanage on Wednesday, 8 April, 1964. The crossover was lifted when Worgret Junction signal box closed in May, 1976 – clay, oil and then finally liquid petroleum gas trains from Furzebrook having to run the final mile into Wareham on the 'down' line. The Standard Class 3 tanks were brief visitors to the Swanage branch during 1964. *Terence Dorrity*

Above: With the driver at the front of the Maunsell push-pull set No. 606 – having received the single-line key token for Corfe Castle from the Worgret Junction signalman – M7 No. 30053 accelerates past the 1885 signal box with the 12.26pm Wareham to Swanage train on Wednesday, 8 April, 1964. No. 30053 escaped the scrapyard after being purchased by an American millionaire for his railway museum in 1964. The Drummond Locomotive Society returned the M7 to Swanage from the USA in 1987 and in 1992 it hauled its first train at Swanage in 28 years. *Terence Dorrity*

Left: LSWR M7 tank No. 30053 leaves the 'down' main line at Worgret Junction as it propels its Maunsell push-pull set No. 606 on the 12.26pm Wareham to Swanage train on Wednesday, 8 April, 1964. The fireman is alone on the footplate as the driver controls the train from the leading coach. No. 30053 was built in London during 1905 to an 1897 design by Dugald Drummond and was based at Bournemouth from 1937. Returning to Bournemouth in late 1963, No. 30053 was withdrawn in May, 1964. *Terence Dorrity*

Above: The driver of a train bound for Corfe Castle catches the single line key token from Worgret Junction signalman Arthur Blick on Saturday, 4 July, 1959. At the rear of the LSWR push-pull carriage set is M7 tank No. 30057 with, in the distance, the bridge carrying the A352 Wareham to Wool road. LSWR push-pull sets were first used experimentally on the Swanage branch in 1912 and regularly from 1922 until the late 1950s. *Trevor Owen/Colour-Rail.com*

Left: Worgret Junction signal box viewed from the branch in April, 1969. In front of the signal box is the wooden platform for the single line key token hoop catcher and net while to the left is an oil lamp providing night-time illumination. Closed in May, 1976, the signal box was demolished in January, 1978. Regular Worgret signalmen during the 1950s and 1960s were Arthur Blick as well as brothers Eddie and Cliff Brown. *Anthony E. Trood*

Above: Worgret Junction signal box interior during April, 1969, showing the 16-lever Stevens frame with, on the block shelf above, the signalling instruments and signal indicators for the double track main line and the single line to Corfe Castle. The Tyer's No. 12 electric key token machine for the line to Corfe Castle can be seen to the left with a healthy supply of key tokens. *Anthony E. Trood*

Left: The Tyer's No. 12 key token machine on Thursday, 9 September, 1965, with a token having been given to the driver of a train to Corfe Castle by signalman Cliff Brown in a leather pouch attached to a hoop. After the single line opened in 1885, trains were signalled under a staff and ticket arrangement. In 1898, Worgret Junction to Corfe Castle was operated under a Tyer's No. 6 tablet machine until 1914 when that changed to a Tyer's No. 7 tablet machine. The Tyer's No. 12 key token machine was introduced in 1961. *Mike Walshaw*

Viewed from Baggs Bridge, Maunsell push-pull set No. 612 is propelled on to the branch by M7 No. 30052 on Sunday, 19 May, 1963. Built at Nine Elms in 1905, No. 30052 was based at Bournemouth in 1931 and for four years from 1948 – returning to Bournemouth in 1963, before being withdrawn in 1964. After closure, Worgret Junction signal box was replaced with a ground frame unlocked by an Annett's Key attached to a single line staff from Wareham signal box. *John Spencer Gilks*

It's 9.50am on Wednesday, 8 April, 1964, and M7 No. 30053 steams under Baggs Bridge on the approach to Worgret Junction with a Maunsell push-pull set No. 606 on the 9.30am from Swanage. No. 30053 has been hauling trains between Swanage, Corfe Castle and Norden Park & Ride on the Swanage Railway since the summer of 1992.
Terence Dorrity

In May, 1966, the fireman leans out as Standard Class '4' 2-6-4 tank No. 80019 climbs the 1 in 80 gradient from the two River Frome bridges to Worgret Junction with five 1940s Bulleid coaches on the 6.17pm from Swanage to Wareham – the returning working of the 5.02pm weekday workers' all stations train from Bournemouth. In the distance, the line sweeps down past the 'up' home signal, over the River Frome water meadows and up the 1 in 78 gradient through East Holme.
Andrew P.M. Wright Collection

Above: With the driver in the front of Maunsell push-pull set No. 606, M7 No. 30053 picks up speed down the 1 in 80 gradient from Worgret Junction towards the two cast iron bridges across the River Frome with the 11.10am to Swanage on Wednesday, 8 April, 1964. The engine has just passed the 'up' home signal for the junction. *Terence Dorrity*

Right: It's 10.50am on Wednesday, 8 April, 1964, and BR Standard Class '3' 2-6-2 tank No. 82028 scurries over one of the two River Frome bridges bound for Worgret Junction with the 10.30am Swanage to Wareham train. Beyond the Maunsell push-pull set No. 609 are the water meadows with East Holme and the Purbeck Hills in the distance. *Terence Dorrity*

Left: Class 33 diesel-electric No. 6536 hauls two 4TC 'push-pull' carriage sets over one of the two River Frome bridges with the 10.47am Swanage to London train on Saturday, 26 July, 1969. With one 4TC set in 1967 BR blue livery – and the other in the new BR blue and grey livery – the train was the return working of the 07.57am London to Swanage. No. 6536 was re-numbered 33 117 in the 1970s and withdrawn in 1993 before being preserved. *Roger Aldous*

Below: Ivatt 2-6-2 tanks No. 41284 and No. 41301 haul the nine-coach Locomotive Club of Great Britain 'Dorset Belle' railtour up the 1 in 78 gradient from the River Frome past East Holme on Sunday, 27 February, 1966. The rear of the train can be seen passing the Worgret Junction distant signal. The line beyond the train was the scene of an accident on Saturday, 19 June, 1886, when a mixed passenger and freight train partially derailed, some of the rake falling down the embankment. Two women and a child on board were slightly injured. *John Spencer Gilks*

Right: Class 33 diesel-electric No. D6507 powers the 9.15am London to Swanage train under the Holme Lane bridge and up the 1 in 78 gradient to Creech and Furzebrook on Saturday, 27 August, 1966. After its arrival at Swanage, the Class 33 worked light engine with Standard Class '4' 2-6-4 tank No.80019 – which itself had shunted No. D6507's carriages into Swanage goods yard – back to Wareham and Bournemouth. No. D6507 was withdrawn in December, 1986. *John R. Coleman*

Below: M7 tank No. 30057 scurries down the 1 in 78 gradient between Creech Bottom and Holme Lane with its Maunsell push-pull set bound for Wareham on Saturday, 9 June, 1962. Maunsell push-pull sets appeared on branch services from 1960. Trains heading for Worgret Junction could reach quite high speeds during the two-mile descent to Worgret Junction – more than the 45mph branch line limit. *Gavin W. Morrison*

Above: Ivatt 2-6-2 tank No. 41312 accelerates up the 1 in 78 gradient from Holme Lane to Furzebrook over the Grange Road bridge at Creech Bottom with a train for Corfe Castle on Saturday, 27 August, 1966, composed of two 1950s Mark One coaches and a 1940s Bulleid open. *John R. Coleman*

Left: 'Crompton' Class 33 diesel-electric No. D6507 hauls a rake of eight Mark One coaches on a London to Swanage train over the Grange Road girder bridge at Creech Bottom during the summer of 1965. The 'Crompton's first operated to Swanage on London trains during 1963 with push-pull equipped Class 33s running through the Isle of Purbeck from the Capital from July, 1967, until October, 1969. *Colin L. Caddy*

Above: The last Swanage branch steam train coasts down the 1 in 78 gradient from Furzebrook and over the farmer's crossing at Creech Bottom bound for Worgret Junction. Rebuilt Battle of Britain class Bulleid Pacific No. 34089 *602 Squadron* is on the rear of the Railway Correspondence and Travel Society's 12-coach 'Farewell to Southern Steam Tour'. This crossing was where the last train to Swanage on the night of Saturday, 1 January, 1972, was nearly held up for charity by occupants from the nearby Lazy C. Ranch dressed in Wild West costumes – the intended stunt being foiled by a last minute tip-off to British Rail. *John R. Coleman*

Right: Standard Class '4' 2-6-4 tank No. 80138 sweeps down the 1 in 78 gradient from Furzebrook towards the Creech Bottom farm crossing with a train to Wareham on Saturday, 11 June, 1966. In tow is the final form of branch line stock before the arrival of the 'Hampshire' diesel-electric multiple units in September, 1966 – a 1950s maroon Mark One open and a 1940s Bulleid brake coach. Against the skyline are the workers' cottages and ball clay works at Furzebrook. *John R. Coleman*

The final steam-hauled Monday to Friday Furzebrook ball clay train runs down the 1 in 78 gradient from the works at lunchtime on Friday, 7 July, 1967 – just three days before the end of steam traction on British Rail's Southern Region – bound for Worgret Junction and the main line. Shorn of its nameplate and two days away from withdrawal, rebuilt West Country class Bulleid Pacific No. 34021 *Dartmoor* will drop off the wagons in Poole yard – to be picked up by an evening freight train from Eastleigh – before returning to Bournemouth light engine. *Michael Hardy*

Crossing the heathland between Stoborough and Creech – and viewed from the overbridge at Furzebrook – Ivatt 2-6-2 tank No. 41224 climbs the 1 in 78 gradient from Creech Bottom with an afternoon train of three Bulleid coaches bound for Corfe Castle and Swanage during the summer of 1966, just a few weeks before the branch service was dieselised on Monday, 5 September. *Michael Hardy*

Above: Viewed through the bridge arch carrying the road to the Blue Pool beauty spot, driver Percy Stone and his 18-year-old fireman Melvyn Cox shunt the final steam-hauled ball clay train from the works of Pike Brothers, Fayle and Company at Furzebrook during the lunchtime of Friday, 7 July, 1967. The siding into the clay works was laid in 1902 – 17 years after the opening of the Swanage branch. Entering Southern Railway service in 1946 and rebuilt in 1957, No. 34021 *Dartmoor* ran almost a million miles before being scrapped at Cashmores of Newport in 1968. *Michael Hardy*

Right: With the Bournemouth fireman looking from the footplate, Ivatt 2-6-2 tank No. 41312 scurries past the Furzebrook ball clay sidings on Saturday, 27 August, 1966, with the 2.30pm from Swanage. The embankment to the left was excavated in 1978 when a rail terminal was built for the export of oil and liquid petroleum gas from the Wytch Farm oil field near Corfe Castle. The first oil train left the terminal in December, 1978, and the last gas train departed in July, 2005. *John R. Coleman*

Above left: West Country class Bulleid Pacific No. 34025 *Whimple* blows off in the siding of Pike Brothers Fayle & Company with loaded ball clay wagons on Friday, 30 June, 1967. In the run-round loop are the newly delivered empty ball clay wagons with Wareham shunter Bert Sansom walking past the rake. Bournemouth driver Percy Stone and his Weymouth freight guard sit on the steps of the brake van while they wait for a Wareham to Corfe Castle 'Hampshire' diesel-electric multiple unit (DEMU) to pass before the shunting operation can be completed. *George M. Moon*

Above right: Having run round its empty ball clay wagons at Furzebrook on Friday, 7 July, 1967, No. 34021 *Dartmoor* prepares to uncouple and move forward before reversing into the siding to pick up loaded ball clay wagons. Crewed by Bournemouth driver Percy Stone and his teenage fireman Melvyn Cox, 'Dartmoor' then pulled out the loaded wagons before attaching them to the empties in the run-round loop and reversing the empties into the siding ahead of departing for Poole yard with the loaded rake. *Michael Hardy*

Left: From the end of Southern Region steam traction on Monday, 9 July, 1967, the Furzebrook ball clay train was covered by the Eastleigh to Dorchester freight worked by a crew from Weymouth depot. In the year that the Boeing 747 commercial airliner made its first flight, a push-pull fitted Class 33 diesel-electric shunts empty ball clay wagons into the works siding on Thursday, 3 July, 1969, before leaving with loaded wagons which can be seen at the far end of the run-round loop. The last Purbeck ball clay train left Furzebrook in the early 1990s when all export switched to lorries. *George M. Moon*

With the ground frame for the Furzebrook ball clay siding in the foreground, three-coach 'Hampshire' DEMU No. 1108 is about to pass under the Furzebrook Road bridge at the start of a two-mile descent to the River Frome at a gradient of 1 in 78. The concrete hut contained a Tyer's No.12 intermediate key token machine for gaining access to the siding – and locking in a clay train so branch trains could still run between Worgret Junction and Corfe Castle – while the eight-lever ground frame was unlocked using a Worgret Junction to Corfe Castle key token. No. 1108 was built in 1957 and withdrawn in 1979. *Tony Jervis*

Having climbed from Corfe Castle for two miles, three-coach 'Hampshire' DEMU No. 1108 nears the summit at 35 mph – with the power controller set to notch No. 7 'flat out' – as it approaches Furzebrook with the 1.48pm from Swanage on Saturday, 22 February, 1969. The half-mile climb from the Catseye A351 bridge and Motala has been at a gradient of 1 in 200. Behind the DEMU is girder bridge No. 10, under which the narrow gauge ball clay tramway ran from Furzebrook to Ridge and Poole Harbour until 1940. *Tony Jervis*

M7 tank No. 30379 climbs the 1 in 80 gradient as it approaches the Catseye A351 road bridge between Corfe Castle and Motala with the 1.33pm from Swanage on Wednesday, 15 August, 1962. In tow is a two-coach 'Ironclad' carriage set with two London-bound through coaches behind – a 1930s Maunsell open and a 1940s Bulleid semi-open brake which will be attached to the 1.25pm Weymouth to London Waterloo train at Wareham. Behind the M7 is Norden Heath with Poole Harbour in the distance. *Tim Stephens*

Looking back towards the Catseye A351 road bridge on Saturday, 27 August, 1966, Ivatt tank No. 41312 coasts down the 1 in 80 gradient from Motala with the 3.22pm from Wareham. Ivatt tanks appeared in late 1963 and took over the branch service in May, 1964 – along with Standard Class '3' 2-6-2 and Class '4' 2-6-4 tanks – when the last M7s were withdrawn. Behind the two 1950s Mark One coaches, a brake composite and an open, is the hamlet of Norden. *John R. Coleman*

M7 No. 30110 climbs the 1 in 80 gradient between Eldon's Siding and the Catseye A351 road bridge with the 12.30pm from Swanage on Wednesday, 15 August, 1962. Hauling a Maunsell push-pull set, the M7 as emerged from the Woodpecker Cutting and crossed bridge No. 13 carrying the branch over the Fayle's Middlebere ball clay tramway. Connecting the Norden clay pits with the southern shores of Poole Harbour at Middlebere, the narrow gauge line was built in 1806 and disused by the First World War. *Tim Stephens*

Push-pull trains could reach quite a speed when running down hill – certainly more than the 45mph branch speed limit. On a falling 1 in 80 gradient from the Catseye A351 bridge, M7 No. 30057 pushes its Maunsell set on the 2.20pm from Wareham out of the Woodpecker Cutting towards the Eldon's ball clay exchange siding north of Corfe Castle on Saturday, 13 April, 1963. The driver has shut the regulator and put on the blower valve to prevent the fire blowing back – hence the wisp of steam from the M7's smokebox. *Alan Wild*

Ivatt tank No. 41224 clatters down the 1 in 80 gradient from Eldon's Siding to the Scotland Heath and Arne road overbridge on Saturday, 11 June, 1966, bound for Corfe Castle. Opened with the branch in May, 1885, Eldon's Siding transferred mined Norden ball clay from narrow gauge to standard gauge wagons for export out of Purbeck. Renamed Norden Siding in September, 1950, Eldon Siding was officially taken out of use in March, 1966. To the right is the Corfe Castle distant signal while behind the first Bulleid coach is the 'whistle' board for a crossing used by road lorries taking out ball clay with the end of Eldon's Siding from the early 1960s. *John R. Coleman*

Looking towards Corfe Castle from the Scotland and Arne road bridge, an unidentified Standard Class '4' 2-6-0 accelerates up the 1 in 80 gradient towards Eldon's Siding with an eight-coach Swanage to London Waterloo train on Thursday, 1 July, 1965. Behind the train is where the Swanage Railway's Norden station was built in 1994 while the access road to the Wytch Farm oil field, and later the station, was built mid-way along the rake of coaches in 1987. *R.C. Riley*

Norden Clay Tramway

Three-coach 'Hampshire' DEMU No. 1123 accelerates past the site of the future Swanage Railway Norden Park & Ride station bound for Wareham on Sunday, 22 June, 1969. To the left is the weighbridge for the 2-foot gauge ball clay tramway while in the distance is the ball clay rail-road lorry drop transfer shed. In operation when the Swanage branch opened in 1885, Norden's narrow gauge railway system was last used during late 1970 with the tracks lifted in 1971. No. 1123 was built in 1959 and withdrawn in 1999 before being preserved. *R.C. Riley*

The rail-road 'lorry drop' at Norden looking south as several narrow gauge wagons of ball clay are dropped into an English China Clays lorry on Friday, 4 July, 1969. On the far side of the corrugated iron shed is the Swanage branch line over which the lorry reversed to reach the loading facility. All that is now left of this charming scene are the two stone abutments for the shed which form the entrance to the Swanage Railway's Norden station opened in August, 1995. To the right, the photographer's father watches an operation that would come to an end just over a year later. *George M. Moon*

Above left: Still carrying the old Pike Brothers, Fayle and Company Limited livery and markings, an English China Clays lorry crosses the branch with ball clay destined for the Furzebrook processing works on Friday, 4 July, 1969. Out of view to the right is the rail-road 'lorry drop' shed where clay in narrow gauge tipper wagons was tipped into lorries. The 'lorry drop' facility came into use in the late 1950s and was closed in late 1970 when the narrow gauge ball clay tramway system at Norden ceased. In the distance is the main A351 Corfe Castle to Wareham road and West Hill of the Purbeck Hills. *George M. Moon*

Above right: An iconic scene from yesteryear at Norden as narrow gauge passes over standard gauge against the background of Corfe Castle's dramatic ruins on Friday, 19 June, 1970. With legendary English China Clays train driver Eli Kitcatt at the controls, 48DL class Ruston and Hornsby diesel locomotive No. 392117 hauls two metal tipper wagons of ball clay from the Norden mines and over the skew-arch bridge spanning the Swanage branch line bound for the rail-road 'lorry drop'. *R.C. Riley*

Left: A view of English China Clays' narrow gauge Norden depot looking east from the Arne and Scotland road bridge on Friday, 12 June, 1970. With the Swanage branch track to the right, Eli Kitcatt shunts several metal tipper wagons loaded with ball clay. On the front of the train is a grey Ruston & Hornsby diesel No. 175413 built in 1936. To the left is a mess hut with a ball clay drying shed beyond while in the distance is the weighbridge and a run-round loop with the rail-road 'lorry drop' shed beyond. The last narrow gauge clay tramway train ran in late 1970 and the two-foot gauge system was torn up for scrap during 1971. The 18/20 horsepower Lister-engined No. 175413 was sold in August, 1972, and exported to Singapore during October of that year. *R.C. Riley*

Above left: A timeless scene in the year man first landed on the moon. Jack Day shunts four-cylinder 48DL class Ruston & Hornsby diesel locomotive No. 392117 at Norden's No. 12 mine in the lea of the Purbeck Hills on Friday, 4 July, 1969. The 48 horsepower chain-driven locomotive with a three-speed gearbox and compression ignition was built at Lincoln in 1956 and sent from new to work on the quadrupling of the east coast main line at Hadley Wood. By the late 1950s, No. 392117 was hauling ball clay trains at Norden. *George M. Moon*

Above right: Passing the ball clay weathering beds on which the Purbeck Mineral and Mining Museum was built some 40 years later, four-cylinder 48DL class Ruston & Hornsby diesel locomotive No. 392117 hauls two metal tipper wagons of ball clay bound for the rail-road 'lorry drop' on Friday, 19 June, 1970. With its distinctive exhausts, made from brass pipes from one of Norden's narrow gauge steam locomotives, No. 392117 was sold into preservation in the early 1970s and resides on the Old Kiln Light Railway near Farnham in Surrey. *R.C. Riley*

Right: The Norden narrow gauge depot viewed from a rake of metal tipper wagons stored in the run-round loop looking west to the Arne and Scotland road bridge on Friday, 12 June, 1970. To the right is the weighbridge – built in late 1947 - with the ball clay drying shed behind. Beyond is the mess hut next to the Purbeck stone bridge through which the line runs to the disused Eldon's Siding. *R.C. Riley*

Above left: Looking from the ball clay lorry crossing west towards the Scotland and Arne road bridge, Standard Class '4' 2-6-4 tank No. 80081 carries a Bournemouth West to Dorchester headcode on an eight-coach empty stock working from Bournemouth to Swanage on Thursday, 29 August, 1963, ahead of the first Saturday morning 'up' London train. Behind the train is the narrow gauge ball clay skip weighbridge and sheds. *Rodney A. Lissenden*

Above right: Again viewed from the ball clay lorry crossing at Norden – but looking east towards Swanage – M7 tank No. 30048 scurries past the future site of the Swanage Railway's Norden Park & Ride station as it propels a Maunsell set to Corfe Castle on Thursday, 29 August, 1963. Beyond the train is the skew-arch narrow gauge clay tramway bridge. *Rodney A. Lissenden*

Left: With Bournemouth fireman Brian Heckford enjoying a cigarette, Standard Class 4 Tank No. 80138 sweeps past the narrow gauge ball clay tramway at Norden on Saturday, 20 August, 1966, with the 3.50pm train from Wareham to Corfe Castle and Swanage. Metal narrow gauge skips lie next to the clay weathering beds while behind the train is the transfer shed where mined ball clay from Norden was transferred from narrow gauge trains to road lorries. This view is now the Swanage Railway's Norden Park & Ride station, opened in 1995, while to the right is the Purbeck Mineral and Mining Museum. *Andrew P.M. Wright Collection*

Standard Class '4' 2-6-4 tank No. 80138 climbs the 1 in 120 gradient up to the skew-arch narrow gauge clay tramway bridge with a train for Wareham on Saturday, 11 June, 1966. The bridge carried the narrow gauge line from the clay mines at Norden across the A351 Wareham to Corfe Castle road and over the Swanage branch to the road transfer shed and Eldon's Siding. Built in the 1950s for hauling commuter trains into London from the east coast, No. 80138 makes light work of its two-coach set – a 1950s Mark One open and a 1940s Bulleid composite brake.
John R. Coleman

M7 No. 30111's driver looks out for the Norden ball clay lorry crossing as the locomotive climbs the gradient from the Corfe Castle viaduct to the skew-arch narrow gauge clay tramway bridge with a train for Wareham during the summer of 1962. The train is made up of an ex-SECR ten compartment strengthening coach – push-pull fitted and kept at Swanage station – and a Maunsell push-pull set. The rear of the train is passing the 'whistle' board for the ball clay lorry loading crossing. *L. Flint/Colour-Rail.com*

An unidentified Ivatt tank pilots an unidentified Class 33 diesel-electric working the 6.28pm Swange to London ten-coach train on Bank Holiday Whit Monday, 7 June, 1965. This double-heading enabled the steam locomotive to be returned to Wareham or Bournemouth without taking up a separate train path. *Colin L. Caddy*

It's the summer of 1966 and Ivatt 2-6-2 tank No. 41295 sweeps down the incline from Norden and over the Corfe Castle viaduct bound for Swanage. The Purbeck stone viaduct spanned the Corfe River and the B3351 road to Studland. Behind the Ivatt is the village's water pumping station with Poole Harbour in the distance. *John Carter*

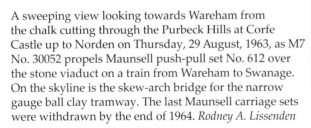

A sweeping view looking towards Wareham from the chalk cutting through the Purbeck Hills at Corfe Castle up to Norden on Thursday, 29 August, 1963, as M7 No. 30052 propels Maunsell push-pull set No. 612 over the stone viaduct on a train from Wareham to Swanage. On the skyline is the skew-arch bridge for the narrow gauge ball clay tramway. The last Maunsell carriage sets were withdrawn by the end of 1964. *Rodney A. Lissenden*

An unidentified Standard Class '4' 2-6-4 tank steams out of Corfe Castle with two 1940s Bulleid carriages bound for Wareham during the summer of 1966. Viewed from the walls of the ruined Medieval castle, to the right of the tall pine trees obscuring the station is the goods shed while in the foreground are the cottages of East Street and the historic water mill. *John Carter*

Back from the beach. Standard Class '4' 2-6-0 No. 76014 accelerates out of the chalk cutting at Corfe Castle with its two 1940s Bulleid coaches on the 6.58pm from Swanage on Sunday, 3 July, 1966. The labourers building the branch during 1884 used gunpowder to blast out the cutting and the explosions caused stones to fall off the Medieval ruins. In August 2012, the remnant of an unexploded gunpowder charge was found in the cutting and made safe by an Army bomb disposal team. *Peter Zabek*

With regular steam ousted eight months previously – and the branch run by 'Hampshire' diesel-electric multiple units – the Locomotive Club of Great Britain's first of two 'Dorset Coast Express' runs to Swanage steams out of Corfe Castle at 2.09pm past the village rooftops bound for Wareham on Sunday, 7 May, 1967. Standard Class '4' 2-6-0 No. 76026 is at the front of the ten-coach train while unrebuilt West Country class Bulleid Pacific No. 34023 *Blackmore Vale* is on the rear. In the foreground is the 18th century Grade Two listed Boar Mill, next to the Byle Brook, which flows under the railway. *John Spencer Gilks*

Trains cross at Corfe Castle on Saturday, 20 August, 1966. Viewed from East Hill, Standard Class '4' 2-6-4 tank No.80019 departs with two 1950s Mark One coaches on the 8.44am from Swanage while Ivatt 2-6-2 tank No. 41230 waits to leave the 'down' platform for Swanage the three 1940s Bulleid coaches on the 8.40am from Wareham. *Peter Zabek*

Viewed from the East Hill of the Purbeck Hills, Standard Class '4' 2-6-4 tank No. 80019 departs Corfe Castle past the village church of St Edward the Martyr with two 1950s Mark One coaches bound for Wareham on Saturday, 20 August, 1966. Behind the train is the station's approach road – with one of the Pullman camping coaches just visible – with the village of Kingston and St James' Church on the skyline. *Roy Hobbs*

Above: Branch and through trains meet at Corfe Castle. M7 tank No. 30667 propels an early evening push-pull train into Corfe Castle from Wareham as rebuilt Battle of Britain class Bulleid Pacific No. 34082 *615 Squadron* waits at the 'up' platform with a train from Swanage to London on Monday, 5 August, 1963. *Alan Trickett*

Left: With rebuilt West Country class Bulleid Pacific No. 34025 *Whimple* at its head, the 9.15am London to Swanage train sweeps into Corfe Castle more than two hours late at 2.21pm on Saturday, 11 June, 1966. Bulleid Pacifics hauled London trains to Swanage from the early 1950s until September, 1966. Built in 1946, No. 34025 was rebuilt in 1957 and withdrawn in July, 1967 – being cut up at Cashmores of Newport in 1968. *John R. Coleman*

Viewed from the Wareham end of Corfe Castle's 'down' platform, a two-coach Maunsell push-pull set No. 612 – with the driver at the front – is propelled past the Medieval castle ruins en route to Swanage on Thursday, 15 August, 1963. Behind the M7 is a non-'push-pull' fitted strengthening coach to cope with the extra summer demand. Before it fell to treachery in a second siege during the English Civil War of the mid-17th Century, Corfe Castle was a fortress, royal palace and prison for more than 600 years.
Kevin Robertson

Above: A charming branch line scene at Corfe Castle on the idyllic summer afternoon of Sunday, 7 July, 1963 – the year American President John F. Kennedy was assassinated. With veteran branch driver Jack Spicer at the far end of the two-coach Maunsell push-pull train, young fireman Keith Sloper from Wareham is at the controls of Victorian-designed M7 tank No. 30108 'Rosie' as it simmers patiently at the 'down' platform while working the 3.15pm Wareham to Swanage train. *Colin L. Caddy*

Right: Making the second of two trips between Swanage and Wareham that day – with sunshine replacing the rain – unrebuilt West Country class Bulleid Pacific No. 34023 *Blackmore Vale* runs into Corfe Castle from Wareham and past the 'down' platform's rotten waiting shelter on the afternoon of Sunday, 7 May, 1967. On the rear of the Locomotive Club of Great Britain's popular 'Dorset Coast Express' rail tour is Bournemouth-based Swanage branch veteran Standard Class '4' tank No. 80011. *John Spencer Gilks*

Corfe Castle station frontage and forecourt in 1951 with the canopy over the booking hall entrance – taken down in the 1950s – and the station master's house beyond. With a Standard Motors car parked in front of the goods shed, box vans and wagons fill the coal and goods shed sidings with camping coach No. 21 near the road entrance to the goods yard. The former 1902 LSWR brake third No. 2753 was broken up in late 1959. *Les Hayward*

Ghosts of times past as Corfe Castle's station frontage decays in June, 1971. To the far left is the signal box, with signalman Arthur Galton's Hillman Minx car, while to the right is the gate leading to the disused goods yard – closed almost six years before – and the site of two Pullman camping coaches. *R. C. Riley*

Corfe Castle station master Richard Walter 'Dicky' Daw and family in the station house garden during 1951. From left are Gwen Hayward, Elsie Maude Daw, aunt Maisie, young cousin Richard on Mr Daw's knee and dogs cocker spaniel Dinah and mongrel Jill. After being senior booking clerk at Swanage, Mr Daw became Corfe Castle station master in 1949. Skilled in Morse code, Mr Daw volunteered as a German radio traffic monitor for the Government's secret Bletchley Park spy complex during the Second World War. *Les Hayward*

The two 1921 Pullman camping coaches – P52 'Milan' with P43 'Coral' behind – in front of the Corfe Castle station on Monday, 30 May, 1966. 'Coral' came to Corfe Castle in 1960 and 'Milan' in 1961. The cost of a weekly stay in the Pullmans during the mid-1960s was £12 and ten shillings. After their last summer season in 1967, the two Pullmans were broken up and burnt where they stood in 1968. *C. L. Caddy*

Right: Summer trains pass at Corfe Castle. With the 'up' starter signal on, a train from Swanage is approaching so Ivatt 2-6-2 tank No. 41316 – with its two 1940s Bulleid coaches in tow – has to wait at the 'down' platform after arriving from Wareham at lunchtime on Monday, 9 May, 1966.
Arthur Wooller via Roger Smith

Below left: Bob Richards operates the 12-lever frame in Corfe Castle signal box and pulls the 'up' starter signal for a train from Swanage on the last night of operation – Saturday, 1 January, 1972. Beginning as a junior porter at Corfe Castle in 1962, Bob moved to Swanage in 1964 as a porter/shunter before returning to Corfe Castle as a leading porter in 1965. He became a signalman in 1967 when the booking office was closed. The signal box was created in 1956 from of an extended porters' lobby on the 'up' platform after the wooden 1885 signal box on the 'down' platform was closed and demolished due to rot and subsidence.
Peter R. Frost

Far right: The interior of Corfe Castle signal box and the Tyer's No. 12 key token machine for the single line to Worgret Junction showing that a train is due to arrive from Wareham on the night of Saturday, 1 January, 1972 – shortly before the final passenger train ran between Swanage, Corfe Castle and Wareham.
Peter R. Frost

Corfe Castle station during the last operating summer of its goods yard before closure as Ivatt 2-6-2 tank No. 41316 prepares to leave the 'down' platform width its wooden waiting shelter with a morning train for Swanage on Thursday, 1 July, 1965. With the end-loading dock to the left, the goods shed and station buildings were built of Purbeck stone in 1884 by Bull & Company of Southampton. *R. C. Riley*

M7 tank No. 30108 'Rosie' propels its Maunsell push-pull set out of Corfe Castle past the goods yard and towards the raised 'down' starter signal on Monday, 13 April, 1963, with the 3.40pm from Wareham. British Railways closed the goods yard on Monday, 4 October, 1965 – the closest rail facilities for freight then being at Wareham. Stockley's the coal merchant kept its stacking ground in the goods yard. *Alan Wild*

With the disused goods yard and headshunt siding to the left, rebuilt West Country class Bulleid Pacific No. 34025 *Whimple* departs Corfe Castle two hours late just before 2.25pm with the eight coach 9.15am train from London on Saturday, 11 June, 1966. The passing loop was lengthened in December, 1943, for troop trains connected with military training in the Isle of Purbeck ahead of the Allied D-Day invasion of France on Tuesday, 6 June, 1944. *John R. Coleman*

A driver's view of the 1 in 80 descent into Corfe Castle from a 'Hampshire' DEMU bound for Wareham on a winter's afternoon in 1966. The train has passed over girder bridge No. 18 at Townsend and the signalman has pulled off the No. 3 'up' home signal, giving the train a clear run into the passing loop and platform. With more than a mile of line from Afflington descending at 1 in 80, drivers could pick up speed to 60 mph by this point – applying the brakes before running over the 15 mph No. 5 point and into the station loop. *Chris Phillips*

Above: With the West Hill of the Purbeck Hills, the ruins of Corfe Castle and the bungalows of Battlemead behind, Ivatt 2-6-2 tank No. 41224 scampers up the 1 in 80 gradient towards the Townsend farmers' crossing bridge with two 1940s Bulleid coaches forming a morning train for Swanage on Tuesday, 7 June, 1966. After the branch's dieselisation on Monday, 5 September, 1966, No. 41224 became the pilot engine at Bournemouth shed until the end of steam on Sunday, 9 July, 1967. *Mike Walshaw*

Left: Climbing at 1 in 80 out of Corfe Castle past Townsend, unrebuilt West Country class Bulleid Pacific No. 34023 *Blackmore Vale* heads the Locomotive Club of Great Britain's ten-coach 'Dorset Coast Express' to Swanage at 1.30pm on Sunday, 7 May, 1967. With Standard Class '4' 2-6-0 No. 76026 on the rear, this was the first of two runs on the branch – the second trip departing Wareham at 3pm with Standard Class '4' 2-6-4 tank No. 80011 on the rear. *John Spencer Gilks*

Right: Ivatt 2-6-2 tank No. 41230 climbs the 1 in 80 gradient south of Corfe Castle on Saturday, 20 August, 1966, as it passes the Townsend farmers' crossing bridge – once known as Common Bridge – and the fixed distant signal for Corfe Castle with a late afternoon train for Swanage. In tow are three 1940s Bulleid coaches which first appeared on branch trains during 1965. As a Corfe Castle junior porter in 1962, Bob Richards cycled along the cinder cess next to the track and climbed the post's ladder to fill the distant signal's oil lamp. *Roy Hobbs*

Below: With Townsend bridge, Corfe Castle village and the Purbeck Hills behind, M7 tank No. 30059 propels Ironclad push-pull set No. 385 – with the driver in the front – on a morning train to Swanage in July, 1959, and is about to pass under the Afflington A351 road bridge. Built at Nine Elms during 1906, No. 30059 was based at Bournemouth in 1931, 1948, 1950 and 1956 – being withdrawn from Bournemouth in 1961 and scrapped at Eastleigh. *J. M. Bairstow/Colour-Rail.com*

Above: With 'Ironclad' push-pull set No. 381 in tow, M7 tank No. 30057 climbs up the 1 in 132 gradient from Woodyhyde to the Afflington A351 road bridge with an early afternoon train from Swanage on Saturday, 27 October, 1962 – during the Cold War international Cuban missile crisis. In the distance are the hills and quarries near Langton Matravers. *Gavin W. Morrison*

Left: Class 33 diesel-electric No. D6507 and Standard Class '4' 2-6-4 tank No. 80019 round the Woodyhyde curve from Harman's Cross and accelerate up the 1 in 132 gradient to the Afflington A351 road bridge on Saturday, 27 August, 1966. The pair is running light engine back to Bournemouth after the Class 33 hauled the 9.15am London to Swanage train while No. 80019 had been on the morning branch service before shunting D6507's eight carriages at Swanage. No. D6507 was withdrawn in December, 1986. *Kevin Robertson*

Above: Having passed under the Haycraft's Lane bridge at Harman's Cross, Ivatt tank No. 41230 coasts down the 1 in 76 gradient towards Quarr Farm with its rake of two 1940s Bulleid coaches bound for Swanage on Saturday, 20 July, 1966 – the day England won the World Cup final against West Germany at Wembley. Beyond the stone bridge is where the Swanage Railway built its second station in 1988, then the first new Dorset station for more than 50 years. *Laurie Golden*

Right: Approaching the Haycraft's Lane bridge, M7 tank No. 30052 and its Maunsell push-pull set climb the 1 in 76 gradient past the village of   Harman's Cross on Sunday, 19 May, 1963, with a train to Corfe Castle. In the distance, beyond the permanent way hut, is the Quarr Farm crossing while to the left are the Purbeck Hills. Built in 1905, No. 30052 was sent to Bournemouth shed in 1931 – returning to the resort in 1948 and 1950. Returning to Bournemouth in 1963, she was withdrawn in 1964. *John Spencer Gilks*

Left: Viewed from the Nursery road bridge carrying the A351 Corfe Castle to Swanage road, three-coach 'Hampshire' DEMU No. 1102 climbs the 1 in 76 gradient towards the Pondarosa Farm crossing before running through the Wilderness wood and past Quarr Farm to Harman's Cross with the 11.45am train from Swanage on Saturday, 8 March, 1969. No. 1102 was built at Eastleigh in 1957 and withdrawn for scrap in 1991. *Roger A. Aldous*

Below: Standard Class '4' 2-6-0 No. 76010 accelerates its two 1940s Bulleid coaches up the 1 in 76 gradient between Herston and New Barn on Sunday, 31 July, 1966, with an afternoon train to Corfe Castle and Wareham. To the left are the trees of Windmill Knap. *Norman Lockett Archive courtesy of David Lockett*

Above left: Ivatt tanks No. 41301 and No. 41284 haul the Locomotive Club of Great Britain's 'Dorset Belle' railtour of nine Mark One coaches over the New Barn bridge and towards the A351 Nursery road bridge on Sunday, 27 February, 1966. The New Barn bridge was subject to a speed restriction and a stream meant the embankment to the right of the bridge was susceptible to slipping – British Railways often sending permanent way trains to pour fine stabilising Meldon Dust ballast down the slope. *Trevor Owen/Colour-Rail.com*

Above right: Viewed from the Washpond Lane bridge looking towards Windmill Knap and New Barn, Standard Class '4' 2-6-4 tank No. 80134 hauls a 1950 BR Mark One open and a 1940s Bulleid brake coach down the 1 in 78 gradient with a train from Corfe Castle on Thursday, 1 April, 1965. *Geoff W.Sharpe*

Standard Class '4' 2-6-4 tank No. 80019 steams under the Washpond Lane bridge – and past the site of the Swanage Railway's Herston Halt opened in 1984 – on Saturday, 20 August, 1966, with two BR 1950s Mark One coaches from Wareham and Corfe Castle on the final mile of its morning journey to Swanage.
Roy Hobbs

Standard Class '4' 2-6-0 No. 76010 accelerates up the 1 in 110 gradient out of Swanage towards the Victoria Avenue road bridge with a two-coach 1940s Bulleid carriage set bound for Corfe Castle and Wareham. Sunday, 21 August, 1966. The Herston side of the road bridge was the location of a headshunt and siding into the Swanage gasworks between 1893 and 1956.
Norman Lockett Archive courtesy of David Lockett

Having brought in a ten-coach excursion train on Monday, 18 May, 1964, unrebuilt West Country class Bulleid Pacific No. 34015 *Exmouth* departs Swanage light engine on the 1 in 110 gradient bound for Bournemouth. In the foreground is the statiion's headshunt while in the distance the line disappears towards the Victoria Avenue road bridge. To the right are the houses of Victoria Avenue and Prospect Crescent with the Purbeck Hills beyond.
Alan Wild

Above: A morning train from Salisbury – via the Avon valley line and the 'Old Road' through West Moors, Wimborne and Broadstone – sweeps into Swanage past the 1885 engine shed in July, 1957, hauled by Standard Class '4' 2-6-0 No. 76005. The engine shed damage was caused when an M7 tank suffered mechanical failure and overshot the turntable. Behind the wooden track gangers' hut, a siding left the headshunt and curved into a stone yard until the late 1940s. *S.C.Townroe/Colour-Rail.com*

Right: Standard Class '3' 2-6-2 tank No. 82027 pulls a rake of ten coaches out of the goods yard at Swanage to release Bulleid Pacific No. 34015 *Exmouth* which had brought an excursion train into the station before the 'West Country' shunted its carriages into the goods yard on Monday, 18 May, 1964. After 'Exmouth' was released from the carriage siding, No. 82027 propelled the stock back into the yard for servicing. *Alan Wild*

With the engine shed now sporting a late 1950s wooden lintel instead of the original arch – which had a pair of wooden doors – fireman Bruce Skitteral is at the controls of Standard Class '4' 2-6-4 tank No. 80146 as it scurries into Swanage with three 1940s Bulleid coaches on a morning train from Wareham during July, 1966. The engine shed closed less than two months later, on the evening of Sunday, 4 September, 1966. *R. C. Riley*

Passing the turntable, water tower and coal stage, Standard Class '4' 2-6-4 tank No. 80019 draws eight coaches from the 9.15am London to Swanage train off a Class 33 diesel-electric locomotive at the far end of the main platform No. 2 on Saturday, 20 August, 1966, before propelling the rake into the goods yard for servicing. No. 80019 and the Class 33 will then run light engine back to Bournemouth. *Peter Zabek*

The coal stage and water tower at Swanage viewed from Court Road during the summer of 1961 as M7 tank No. 30105 is watered and topped up with coal. Built in 1905, No. 30105 was sent to Bournemouth in 1931 before returning in 1951 – staying there until withdrawn and scrapped at Eastleigh in June, 1963.
John Carter

A rare Western Region visitor to Swanage from the Somerset and Dorset line viewed from a train departing the bay platform No.1 in the summer of 1964. Driver Johnny Walker watches his fireman on the tender of green Standard Class '4' 4-6-0 No. 75007 while the locomotive is watered at the coal stage. A Class 33 diesel-electric stands at the main platform No. 2 after taking the carriages off No. 75007 and shunting them into the goods yard. The Class 33 and No. 75007 will return light engine to Bournemouth. *Chris Phillips*

Above: Swanage station's water tower, turntable and engine shed viewed through the Northbrook Road bridge on Monday, 18 May, 1964. Built by the Brown & Bobby engineers of London, the water tower dated from the opening of the line in May, 1885. The tracks to the goods shed, goods yard and carriage sidings are in the foreground. In the distance, the 'home' signal for the main platform No. 2 shows that a train from Corfe Castle is on its way. *Alan Wild*

Left: Ivatt 2-6-2 tank No. 41224 sweeps into Swanage under the Northbrook Road bridge bound for the bay platform No. 1 during the summer of 1965. Swanage driver Fred Norman prepares to hand the hoop and pouch containing the single line tablet from Corfe Castle to the signalman. Preferring the Ivatts to the larger Standard Tanks, Fred later worked the Weymouth to Waterloo line and retired from British Rail at Bournemouth in the early 1990s after driving the first Inter-city 125 high speed train from Poole. *Chris Phillips*

Right: Veteran branch driver Jock Habgood prepares to give the pouch containing the single line tablet from Corfe Castle to the Swanage signalman as Standard Class '3' 2-6-2 tank No. 82027 runs in with the 12.26pm from Wareham on Monday, 18 May, 1964 – the start of the first week without the old M7 tanks. Because the locomotive is not push-pull fitted, it will run round its Maunsell set via the station loop. In the goods yard to the left is the rear of a ten-coach excursion train. *Alan Wild*

Below: M7 tank No. 30379 blows off as it departs Swanage with a morning train for Wareham on Sunday, 26 August, 1962. Behind the M7 is an unusual push-pull set of a former SECR coach and a Maunsell coach. Built at Nine Elms during 1904, No. 30379 was sent to Bournemouth in 1948 and 1950 – returning to Bournemouth in 1961 before being withdrawn and scrapped at Eastleigh in 1963. In the foreground is the station allotment, tended for many years by branch driver Jack Spicer. *Roy Hobbs*

Above: Having been coaled and watered on shed at Swanage, M7 tank No. 30105 reverses into the main platform No. 2 during the summer of 1961 – the driver reaching down to catch the hoop with leather pouch containing the single line tablet for Corfe Castle from signalman Arthur Galton. A rake of 1940s Bulleid carriages from a through train stands in the run-round loop beyond the signal box while several British Railways Bedford delivery lorries are parked under the goods shed canopies. *John Carter*

Left: Swanage signalman Jimmy Hunt stands on the balcony of his box during the summer of 1966. Viewed from Gilbert Road, behind the signal box is the siding to the goods shed, the Second World War air raid shelter and the four long sidings. Closed on Tuesday, 6 June, 1967, the signal box was demolished in late 1967 with the 23-lever frame sold for scrap to Channel Metals of Poole. *Chris Phillips*

Above: Signalman Jimmy Hunt has caught the hoop attached to the leather pouch containing the single line tablet from Corfe Castle from the fireman of rebuilt Battle of Britain class Bulleid Pacific No. 34060 *25 Squadron* as it arrives at Swanage with a train from London during the summer of 1965. To the left is the starting signal for the bay platform No. 1 while to the right is the run-round loop for the main platform No. 2. *Chris Phillips*

Right: A dramatic double-headed departure from Swanage on a summer evening in 1965 as Ivatt tank No. 41314 pilots a Standard Class '4' tank past the signal box with the 6.28pm for Corfe Castle and Wareham. Having brought in the 5pm workers' train from Bournemouth, the Standard Tank was returning to Bournemouth while the Ivatt tank was also Bournemouth-bound, having been one of two locomotives working the branch's two-train summer service: one manned by a Swanage crew and the other by a Bournemouth crew. *Chris Phillips*

Above: M7 tank No. 30105 is about to depart the main platform No. 2 for Wareham during August, 1960, while a Class '4' 2-6-0 waits to shunt a rake of six coaches into the main platform ahead of a departure for Southampton Terminus via the 'Old Road'. In the bay platform No. 1, two BR Mark One coaches wait to form the next morning's through coaches to Wareham for the 'Royal Wessex' London train while the station's coal wagon and eight Maunsell coaches are stabled in the goods yard. *Andrew P.M. Wright Collection*

Left: Bournemouth driver Fred Dunstall makes sure that rebuilt West Country class Bulleid Pacific No. 34005 *Barnstaple* is well oiled before its leaves the main platform No. 2 with the 11.20am train for London on Saturday, 20 August, 1966. On the footplate, 18-year-old fireman Melvyn Cox has let the safety valve 'whimper' at 250 psi, much to the excitement of children watching from Gilbert Road. In the foreground is the line into the bay platform No. 1. Fred retired in the late 1960s. *Chris Phillips*

The interior of Swanage signal box on Tuesday, 7 September, 1965, when signalman Jimmy Hunt was on duty. Opening with the line in May, 1885, the box had a 23-lever Stevens frame and, in 1965, had one spare lever and four push-pull levers. In the far corner is a Tyer's No. 6 electric tablet instrument for the line to Corfe Castle while above the block shelf is the diagram showing the mechanical and electrical locking. *Mike Walshaw*

Signalman Jimmy Hunt prepares to signal a train in 1965. He joined British Railways at Swanage in 1949 as a porter, becoming a porter/shunter, porter/signalman and then a Corfe Castle and Swanage signalman by 1957 – working overtime as a train guard. Offered a main line guard's job at Bournemouth ahead of the signal box closure in June, 1967, Jimmy was unwilling to move his young family out of Swanage and left British Rail in March, 1967, to become a taxi driver. *Chris Phillips*

The Tyer's No. 6 electric tablet instrument No. 30 dating from September, 1898, when the staff and ticket signalling system dating from the branch's opening in May, 1885, was abolished. The machine was used until Tuesday, 6 June, 1967, when Swanage signal box closed. Bought from British Rail by an enthusiast, the machine was stored for more than 30 years and returned to the Swanage Railway's new Swanage signal box when it opened in 2003. *Chris Phillips*

In front of the signal box stove in 1965, signalman Jimmy Hunt with one of the single line tablets – No. 28 made of steel with a brass outer band – for Swanage to Corfe Castle. Jimmy also holds leather pouch in which the tablet is carried before being handed to the crew of a departing locomotive. The other regular Swanage signalmen were Arthur Galton, Bob Inman and Arthur Meehan with one of the relief signalmen being Frank Kitcatt who also lived in Swanage. *Chris Phillips*

Above: Passengers board a train for Wareham during the summer of 1961. Behind M7 tank No. 30105 is a former SECR ten compartment coach behind with a two-coach crimson LSWR push-pull set under the station canopy. In the run-round loop is a rake of 1940s Bulleid coaches from a through train. Because the M7s were push-pull operated – and did not need to run round their stock at Swanage – the loop was often used for stabling carriages for through trains. *John Carter*

Left: Victorian-designed London and South Western Railway M7 No. 30108 'Rosie' in the bay platform No. 1 on Tuesday, 25 June, 1963, before Fred Norman drives her on the 5.38pm train to Corfe Castle and Wareham. Taken from the yard, the goods shed is out of view to the left but its siding is in the foreground while an internal user grounded box van is to the right. *Geoff Rixon*

Above: You can almost smell the bracing sea air and warm lubricating oil – and hear the weary panting of the Westinghouse compressed air pump for the push-pull equipment – as M7 No. 30108 'Rosie' simmers in the bay platform No. 1 at Swanage on Tuesday, 25 June, 1963, before departing with the 5.38pm train to Wareham. In the background is the Railway Hotel with branch driver Fred Norman chatting to passengers while a Duple-bodied Bedford SB coach is parked in the station yard. *Geoff Rixon*

Right: The 1938 Southern Railway extension to Swanage station on Friday, 6 August, 1971, from outside the 1885 station master's house built by Bull & Company of Southampton. From the left is the station master's sitting room, parcels office, booking office, booking hall, bookstall, luggage gates, waiting room, toilets and staff room. The station was purchased from British Rail by Swanage Urban District Council in March, 1974, with Swanage Railway volunteers gaining access to the boarded up building in 1976. *Mike Walshaw*

Above: The station foreman's office next to the bay platform No. 1 and Swanage yard during June, 1967. Built of corrugated iron, it was used by station foreman Jack Cannons from 1963 until the departure of the last station master Harry Newman by 1966 when Jack moved to the station master's office at the far end of the station building. Jack Cannons was made redundant in October, 1969, while his office survived the closure of the line in 1972 – only to be demolished with the platform in July, 1974. *Mike Walshaw*

Above: Swanage station staff outside the parcels office in June, 1965. From left are porter/shunter George Sims, porter Tom Titley, signalman Arthur Galton, station foreman Jack Cannons, porter Bill 'Taffy' Hazell and porter/shunter Bob Richards. When the branch line closed in January, 1972, the only members of Swanage station staff left to be made redundant were porters George Sims and Bill 'Taffy' Hazell as well as booking clerk Maurice Walton. *Chris Phillips*

Left: Escorted by Swanage's last station master Harry Newman, Miss World 1964 – Ann Sidney from Poole – walks past the parcels office after her train journey from Wareham on Thursday, 10 June, 1965, to open the town's annual lifeboat fair. After uncoupling the locomotive from the carriages, porter/shunter Bob Richards got a shock when he looked up at the platform and saw Miss World! Mr Newman had moved to Brockenhurst by the summer of 1966, en route to Winchester. *Bryan Green*

Bournemouth driver Bert Goodridge stands next to his M7 No. 30379 under the 1938 station canopy on Wednesday, 14 June, 1961, as fireman Reuben Hendicott looks from the footplate. The M7 arrived pushing a two-coach push-pull set – LSWR driver brake third No. 2620 and ex-SECR ten-compartment third No. 1066 – and pulling two main line 1940s Bulleid through coaches from London picked up at Wareham. Built at Nine Elms in 1904, No. 30379 was first based at Bournemouth in 1948. It returned in 1950 and 1961 – being withdrawn from Tunbridge Wells West in 1963 and scrapped at Eastleigh. *Cliff Woodhead*

The rarely photographed 'beach end' of the main platform and run-round loop at Swanage viewed from the stopblocks during August, 1966 – the last month of steam traction before the switch to cheaper diesel-electric multiple units. On the embankment, among the flowers, 'Swanage' can just be made out in white-washed stones – a long-time tradition. Swanage station staff continued to win British Rail Southern Region best kept station awards up to 1971. *Andrew P.M. Wright Collection*

Above: Booking office clerk Bryan Green stamps an Edmondson ticket at Swanage before giving it to a passenger in March, 1965. Joining British Railways at Swanage in 1953 as a booking clerk, Bryan worked at Bournemouth's West and Central stations before returning to Swanage. He left in November, 1967, to work in a local betting shop, because of the branch line rundown, reduced booking office hours and the lack of overtime. Trains did not run on winter Sundays from late 1967. *Chris Phillips*

Above: Bournemouth driver Eric Warr gently eases his rebuilt West Country class Bulleid Pacific No. 34009 *Lyme Regis* towards the stopblocks of the main platform No. 2 at Swanage with an eight-coach Sunday ramblers' special in May, 1965. Under the station canopy is the bookstall run by Harold Cook, first for W.H. Smith and then himself. After leaving the carriages in the goods yard, the Bulleid will run to Bournemouth for servicing before returning to Swanage in the afternoon. Built for the Southern Railway in 1945, 'Lyme Regis' was rebuilt in 1961 and withdrawn in 1966 – being scrapped at Buttigiegs of Newport in late 1967. *Chris Phillips*

Right: Swanage station between trains viewed from Gilbert Road on the summer afternoon of Sunday, 7 July, 1963. The green arch-roofed corrugated iron hut was the office for station foreman Jack Cannons. Carriage stock for trains to London – as well as now classic road coaches – are parked in the yard while the branch strengthening coach is berthed at the stopblock end of the run-round loop. Beyond are the distinctive gables of the Railway Hotel while to the right is the large goods shed. *Colin L. Caddy*

The fireman of unrebuilt West Country class Bulleid Pacific No. 34015 *Exmouth* chats to an enthusiast at the end of the long No. 2 carriage siding at Swanage on Monday, 18 May, 1964. The Bulleid Pacific had brought in a ten-coach excursion train and was waiting to be released by Standard Class '3' 2-6-2 tank No. 82027 after it arrived with the 12.26pm train from Wareham. Behind the locomotive are the chimneys of the station master's house while in the foreground is Purbeck stone belonging to mason Thomas Hancock. *Alan Wild*

Another view of unrebuilt West Country class Bulleid Pacific No. 34015 *Exmouth* as it simmers at the town end of Swanage station's long carriage siding No. 2 on Monday, 18 May, 1964. Behind is the roof of the Railway Hotel in Rempstone Road while to the right are the sheds of stonemason Thomas Hancock in King's Road. *Alan Wild*

Above: Rebuilt West Country class Bulleid Pacific No. 34009 *Lyme Regis* prepares to draw its eight carriages out of siding No. 2 at Swanage before shunting it into the main platform No. 2 ahead of the Sunday ramblers' special return working home in May, 1965. Behind the locomotive is the goods shed built in 1884 and extended in 1898. *Chris Phillips*

Left: Swanage station yard on Thursday, 17 August, 1961, as Standard Class '4' 2-6-0 No. 76015 pauses while shunting. Swanage and Corfe Castle goods yards were closed on Monday, 4 October, 1965, with the nearest rail freight collection point being Wareham. To the left is the signalman's Ford Prefect car while to the right is the loading gauge and former weighbridge building demolished during July, 1974. In the foreground is the stacking yard of Stockley's coal merchants. *George M. Moon*

Arrival of the Diesels

Above: It's a Sunday in August, 1966, and Standard Class '4' 2-6-0 No. 76010 leaves bay platorm No. 1 at Swanage with two 1940s Bulleid carriages on the 5.57pm to Wareham. In the main platform No. 2, Brush Type 4 Class 47 diesel-electric No. D1690 waits to depart with the eight-coach 6.12pm summer Sundays return stopping train to Eastleigh. The Class 47 still carries its tail lamp after running light engine from Bournemouth and retrieving the stock from the goods yard at Swanage. *Chris Phillips*

Right: Class 33 diesel-electric No. D6507 runs into Swanage with the 9.15am train from London at 12.35pm on Saturday, 27 August, 1966. In the headshunt siding near the advanced starter signal, Standard Class '4' 2-6-4 tank No. 80019 waits to pull the eight coaches off D6507 in the main platform No. 2 and shunt them into the carriage sidings. No. D6507 and No. 80019 will both return to Bournemouth light engine. *Colin L. Caddy*

Above: Class 33 diesel-electric No. D6507 and Standard Class '4' 2-6-4 tank No. 80019 run light engine back to Bournemouth on the afternoon of Saturday, 27 August, 1966, and accelerate up the 1 in 80 gradient between the Woodpecker Cutting and the Catseye A351 road bridge between Corfe Castle and Motala. The Class 33 hauled the 9.15am London to Swanage train while No. 80019 had been on the morning branch service before shunting D6507's eight carriages at Swanage. No. D6507 was withdrawn in 1986. *John R. Coleman*

Above: A Bournemouth crew at Swanage – driver Reg Sparey and fireman Brian Heckford in the yard with Class 33 diesel-electric No. D6535 in August, 1965. The pair had arrived with a London train and shunted the stock into carriage siding No. 2 before No. D6535 returned to Bournemouth light engine or on the front of a service train. One of several Class 33s converted during 1966 and 1967 for push-pull working between Bournemouth and Weymouth – and the Swanage branch – from Monday, 10 July, 1967, No. D6535 was withdrawn in 1998 and preserved. Brian started at Bournemouth in 1960 and retired from the depot in 2010. *Chris Phillips*

Left: Viewed from the signal box balcony, Class 33 No. D6533 departs the main platform No.2 with a train for London during the summer of 1966. The train was signalled with a green flag as its eight coaches fouled the track circuit so the starting signal at the end of the platform could not be operated. *Chris Phillips*

Above: In the cab of Brush Type 4 Class 47 diesel-electric No. D1718, Bournemouth driver Percy Green prepares to leave Swanage with the 6.12pm summer Sundays return stopping train to Eastleigh during July, 1966. Because the Swanage branch closure created a surplus of drivers at Bournemouth depot, senior long-serving Percy Green, Johnny Walker and Reg Hyder retired in March, 1972. Through the cab window is signalman Jimmy Hunt's black Ford Prefect car.

Top right: Swanage porter/shunter George Sims watches as Brush Type 4 Class 47 diesel-electric No. D1718 draws its eight-coach rake out of the closed goods yard during July, 1966, before hauling the 6.12pm summer Sundays return stopping train to Eastleigh. The goods shed road and the far sidings have been lifted. The remaining sidings were lifted during late 1967. Behind George is the Second World War air raid shelter demolished in July, 1974.

Right: Brush Type 4 Class 47 diesel-electric No. D1718 throbs at the head of its eight-coach 6.12pm summer Sundays return stopping train to Eastleigh in the main platform No. 2 at Swanage during July, 1966. In the bay platform No. 1, Standard Class '4' 2-6-0 No. 76010 waits to leave with the two-coach 5.57pm train for Wareham while the track to the goods shed is in the process of being lifted. *All Chris Phillips*

Above: Viewed from the signal box balcony, Brush Type 4 Class 47 diesel-electric No. D1718 waits for the green flag from the Swanage signalman before departing for Eastleigh at 6.12pm during July, 1966. The train was started with a green flag as its eight coaches fouled the track circuit so the starting signal at the end of the platform could not be operated. In front of the Class 47 is the space-saving double-slip, two track points in one. The branch train – a Standard Class '4' 2-6-0 No. 76010 and two coaches – waits to depart from the bay platform No. 1. *Chris Phillips*

Left: After bringing in carriages to Swanage on Friday, 14 August, 1965, for a Saturday train to London the next morning, Class 33 diesel-electric No. D6530 has left the coach set in the goods yard before waiting for a path back to Bournemouth light engine or on the front of a passenger train. With an Eastleigh driver at the controls of No. D6530, to the right is a permanent way hut made of old wooden sleepers with a track gangers' sharpening stone outside for maintaining tools. No. D6530 was withdrawn in 1988 and preserved. *Colin L. Caddy*

Sunset of Branch Steam

Swanage signalman Jimmy Hunt is about to give the crew of rebuilt West Country class Bulleid Pacific No. 34040 *Crewkerne* the single line tablet for Corfe Castle before Bournemouth driver Bill Hayward and fireman Peter Trim depart with the 11.20am eight-coach train to London Waterloo on Saturday, 27 August, 1966. The Bournemouth crew will be relieved at Bournemouth by Nine Elms men for the remaining journey to the Capital. *Alan Wild*

Teenage Bournemouth fireman Melvyn Cox allows the safety valve of rebuilt West Country class Bulleid Pacific No. 34005 *Barnstaple* to 'whimper' at 250 psi in readiness for the departure from Swanage with the 11.20am train to London on Saturday, 20 August, 1966, that will take three hours to reach the Capital. Viewed from behind the signal box, the bay platform No. 1 starting signal on its gantry dominates the scene while the track to the disused goods shed has been lifted. No. 34005 was withdrawn at the end of the 1966 summer service but re-instated for Christmas parcels traffic and then withdrawn. *Chris Phillips*

Above: Standard Class '4' 2-6-4 tank No. 80019 departs the bay platform No. 1 on Saturday, 20 August, 1966, with the 12.40pm to Wareham after the arrival of the eight-coach 9.15am from London into the main platform No. 2 – hauled by a Class 33 diesel-electric locomotive. After No. 80019 clears station limits, fellow Standard Tank No. 80011 in the goods yard will pull the stock off the Class 33 and shunt the carriages into the goods yard. No. 80011 and the Class 33 will then return to Bournemouth light engine. *Roy Hobbs*

Left: Rebuilt West Country class Bulleid Pacific No. 34005 *Barnstable* with driver Fred Dunstall at the controls – and young fireman Melvyn Cox still short of steam – climbs up the 1 in 76 gradient between Quarr Farm and the Haycraft's Lane bridge at Harman's Cross on Saturday, 20 August, 1966, with the eight-coach 11.20am Swanage to London Waterloo which pulled into the Capital just before 3pm. *Roy Hobbs*

Viewed from Wareham's north bay platform No. 4, Standard Class '4' 2-6-0 No. 76014 accelerates its two 1940s Bulleid coaches out of the 'down' south bay platform No. 1 on a summer evening in 1966 bound for Worgret Junction and the start of the single line to Corfe Castle and Swanage. To the right is the 'Up Siding West' used for berthing spare branch coach sets. *Bob Bishop*

An atmospheric branch line scene as regular steam traction on the branch enters its final weeks. Standard Class '4' 2-6-0 No. 76014 climbs up the 1 in 80 gradient from Corfe Castle to the Afflington A351 road bridge with its two 1940s Bulleid coaches on the 7.44pm train from Wareham during the balmy summer evening of Sunday, 3 July, 1966. *Peter Zabek*

Above: Standard Class '4' 2-6-0 No. 76010 at Swanage with two 1940s Bulleid coaches on Sunday, 24 August, 1966, waits for its next departure for Corfe Castle and Wareham – five weeks before it formed the last regular steam train on the branch on Sunday, 4 September, 1966. The curved-roofed station foreman's office is to the right and beyond the stopblocks is the Railway Hotel. Swanage station was gas lit until the end in 1972. *Norman Lockett Archive courtesy of David Lockett*

Left: With the narrow gauge railway system for the Norden ball clay mines to the left – and viewed from the Scotland and Arne road bridge – Standard Class '4' 2-6-0 No. 76014 accelerates its two 1940s Bulleid coaches up the 1 in 80 gradient away from Corfe Castle and is approaching Eldon's Siding with an early evening train to Wareham during the summer of 1966. *Bob Bishop*

Branch Steam's Last Weekend

Standard class '4' 2-6-4 tank No. 80134 stands below the Medieval ruins at Corfe Castle before departing for Wareham on the morning of Saturday, 3 September, 1966. With the signalman having pulled the 'up' starter signal, the line is clear to Worgret Junction. Standard Class '4' 2-6-4 tanks first appeared on the Swanage branch during the summer of 1963 as the number of M7 tanks declined. *Colin L. Caddy*

On the morning of Saturday, 3 September, 1966, Ivatt 2-6-2 tank No. 41316 sits at Corfe Castle's down platform while running light engine to Swanage. The locomotive is waiting for Standard class '4' 2-6-4 tank No. 80134 to arrive with an 'up' train from Swanage. Behind is the stationmaster's house, first occupied by Hubert Owen Green when the line opened in May, 1885. The last stationmaster was Bill Smith who had moved to Broadstone by the end of 1965. The house was occupied by Swanage station foreman Jack Cannons from 1966 until the mid-1970s. *Colin L. Caddy*

Rebuilt West Country class Bulleid Pacific No. 34004 *Yeovil* shunts eight coaches for the 9.38am to London into the main platform No. 2 at Swanage on Saturday, 3 September, 1966. Calling at Corfe Castle, Wareham, Poole, Bournemouth and Southampton, the train reached London Waterloo at 12.49pm. Driver Les Oliver and fireman Ricky Savage of Bournemouth depot admire the view while above are the home signals for the main and bay platforms.
John R. Coleman

The end of an era and one of the last occasions that carriage stock is shunted by a steam locomotive in the goods yard at Swanage. Standard Class '4' 2-6-4 tank No. 80138 pauses next to a rake of Bulleid coaches on the morning of Saturday, 3 September, 1966. Behind the locomotive is the loading gauge and former weighbridge building. Beyond is the brick Second World War air raid shelter, behind the signal box, and the Northbrook Road bridge. *Colin L. Caddy*

Last Evening of Branch Steam

The last day of regular Swanage branch steam traction was Sunday, 4 September, 1966. The last summer Sundays 6.12pm Swanage to Eastleigh train on 4 September, 1966, was not hauled by a Class 47 diesel-electric but by Standard Class '4' 2-6-4 tank No. 80140. With the home signal for Worgret Junction behind the train, No. 80140 approaches the curve to the main line ahead of the remaining almost two-hour journey to Eastleigh. *Alan Trickett*

Standard Class '4' 2-6-0 No. 76010 climbs up the 1 in 80 gradient from the Frome River to Worgret Junction with the 5.57pm train from Swanage. No. 76010 hauled the last steam branch train of the day – the 8.14pm from Swanage and the 9pm from Wareham back to Swanage before running empty back to Bournemouth. The driver was former Branksome shed and then Bournemouth depot-based Johnny Walker who drove the last steam train on the Somerset & Dorset line in March, 1966. *Alan Trickett*

'Hampshire' DEMU Arrival

Above: Three-coach 'Hampshire' DEMU No. 1108 under Swanage station's 1938 canopy, last painted in 1954, before departing for Wareham during early September, 1966. The closure of the Fawley branch and the demise of the Horsham to Brighton line in February and March, 1966, released 'Hampshire' DEMUs for Swanage branch service. The black triangle on the motor coach shows the unit's guard compartment. *Chris Phillips*

Left: By June, 1966, British Rail posters told passengers that steam trains would be replaced by ' modern' 'Hampshire' class diesel-electric multiple units (DEMUs) from Monday, 5 September, 1966 – the first being the 6.50am from Swanage. Despite the new service, Southern Region managers wanted to close the Swanage branch from June, 1966. *Tim Stephens*

Right: The timetable given to passengers during the summer of 1966 showing train times being altered so the branch could be operated by one Southern Region 'Hampshire' DEMU and working costs considerably reduced. British Rail advertised its first intention to close the line on Wednesday, 18 October, 1967. *Danny Hathaway*

REVISED TRAIN SERVICE
SWANAGE BRANCH LINE

From MONDAY, 5 SEPTEMBER, the existing weekday steam services between WAREHAM and SWANAGE will be withdrawn and replaced by a modern diesel electric multiple unit service.

Please ask at this station for leaflet giving train timings.

British Rail | Southern Region

Revised Train Service
Swanage Branch

From Monday, 5 September, the existing weekday steam service between Wareham and Swanage will be withdrawn and replaced by a modern diesel-electric multiple unit service. Trains will run at the following times:

WAREHAM	dep.	07 16	08 11	09 11	10 09	11 15
CORFE CASTLE	dep.	07 27	08 22	09 22	10 20	11 26
SWANAGE	arr.	07 36	08 31	09 31	10 29	11 35
					A SO	
WAREHAM	dep.	12 16	13 18	14 15	15 40	
CORFE CASTLE	dep.	12 27	13 29	14 26	15 51	
SWANAGE	arr.	12 36	13 38	14 35	16 00	
		SX	B SO			
WAREHAM	dep.	15 44	16 00	17 03	17 55	18 48
CORFE CASTLE	dep.	15 55	16 11	17 14	18 06	18 59
SWANAGE	arr.	16 04	16 20	17 23	18 15	19 08
WAREHAM	dep.	19 44	21 27			
CORFE CASTLE	dep.	19 55	21 38			
SWANAGE	arr.	20 04	21 47			

SWANAGE	dep.	06 50	07 40	08 35	09 35	10 34
CORFE CASTLE	dep.	06 59	07 49	08 44	09 44	10 43
WAREHAM	arr.	07 10	08 00	08 55	09 55	10 54
SWANAGE	dep.	11 40	12 40	13 42	14 45	
CORFE CASTLE	dep.	11 49	12 49	13 51	14 54	
WAREHAM	arr.	12 00	13 00	14 02	15 05	
		A SO	SX	B SO		
SWANAGE	dep.	16 06	16 22	16 25	17 27	18 19
CORFE CASTLE	dep.	16 15	16 31	16 34	17 36	18 28
WAREHAM	arr.	16 26	16 42	16 45	17 47	18 39
SWANAGE	dep.	19 13	20 24			
CORFE CASTLE	dep.	19 22	20 33			
WAREHAM	arr.	19 33	20 44			

SO Sats. only.
SX Sats. excepted.
A Until 15 October, 1966 and from 1 April, 1967.
B From 22 October, 1966 to 25 March, 1967.

British Rail | Southern Region

Published by British Rail, Southern Region AD 923/A10/6966
Frederick Printing Co. Ltd. E.C.2

'Hampshire' DEMU No. 1108 waits in the 'down' south bay platform No.1 at Wareham before departing for Swanage on Sunday, 19 March, 1967. Stabled nightly at Bournemouth station's middle siding No. 1 – and refuelled at the Bournemouth West depot – the units travelled to Eastleigh for changing every Wednesday night. It was not until the end of main line steam on Monday, 9 July, 1967, that the '03' Swanage branch service headcode for diesel workings was replaced by the '98' headcode which lasted until the last day of trains to Swanage. *John R. Coleman*

A very unusual visitor at Swanage on Sunday, 2 July, 1967. Southern Region three-coach 'Tadpole' diesel-electric multiple unit No. 1201 at the main platform No. 2, having arrived with the 7.44pm train from Wareham. In the distance, branch driver Fred Norman chats to the guard before departing with the 8.24p last train of the day to Wareham. Comosed of two narrow-bodied 'Hastings' DEMU coaches and one normal width 'Hampshire' DEMU coach, the 'Tadpole' replaced a failed 'Hampshire' DEMU for the day. Introduced from early 1965, it was very rare to see 'Tadpole's operating away from the Reading to Tonbridge line for which they were built. No. 1201 was disbanded in 1979. *Chris Phillips*

End of Steam Specials

Above: The Locomotive Club of Great Britain's 'Dorset Belle' rail tour visited Swanage from London on Sunday, 27 February, 1966, and arrived in the resort at 12.54pm. Started with a green flag from signalman Arthur Galton because the long train fouled the track circuits, Ivatt tanks No. 41301 and No. 41284 depart Swanage with the 'Dorset Belle' at 1.10pm after a 16-minute stay in the town. Workmen installing new galvanised point rodding throughout the station watch the departure. Less than two years later, the signal box would be demolished with the signalling - and the new point rodding - being ripped out for scrap. *Roy Brough*

Left: By the 'down' home signal gantry next to the Swan Brook bridge and King George's Field, Ivatt tanks No. 41284 and No. 41301 prepare to run round their nine-coach train with the help of station porter/shunter George Sims. As part of the manoeuvre, No. 41284 is signalled into the goods yard. After leaving Swanage, the 'Dorset Belle' paused at Corfe Castle for a seven minute photographic stop at 1.22pm before going on to the Bridport branch. *Michael Hardy*

Ivatt 2-6-2 tank No. 41320 on the Manchester Rail Travel Society's 'Hants and Dorset Branch Flyer' draws attention at Swanage on Saturday, 25 March, 1967. Arriving at 4.45pm and running round its five coaches, the Ivatt prepares to depart for Wareham. Telling photographers to keep off the signal posts, relief signalman Frank Kitcatt is in the signal box and the carriage sidings are empty. By the end of 1967, the signal box was demolished and all tracks, except the running line, lifted. *Chris Phillips*

A dismal air of decay and disuse matching the dull and depressing weather on Saturday, 25 March, 1967. Having run on freight lines to Broadstone and Blandford Forum earlier in the afternoon – and spending 15 minutes at Swanage – the rail tour departs at 5pm. After a six-minute stop at Corfe Castle, the train passed Worgret Junction at 5.25pm en route to Bournemouth and Southampton. With 'Hampshire' DEMUs operating the branch service, the surplus unused tracks wait to be lifted. *Chris Phillips*

Above: The second run to Swanage for the Locomotive Club of Great Britain's 'Dorset Coast Express' rail tour as it departs Corfe Castle after arriving at 2.43pm on Sunday, 7 May, 1967. On the front of the ten-coach train is unrebuilt West Country class Bulleid Pacific No. 34023 *Blackmore Vale* with Standard Class '4' 2-6-4 tank No. 80011 on the back. *John Spencer Gilks*

Left: Viewed from the end-loading dock and looking across the disused goods yard at Corfe Castle, the 'Dorset Coast Express' runs in from Swanage at 3.25pm on Sunday, 7 May, 1967, with Standard Class '4' 2-6-4 tank No. 80011 on the front and unrebuilt West Country class Bulleid Pacific No. 34023 *Blackmore Vale* on the rear of the ten-coach train. Corfe Castle's goods yard closed on Monday, 4 October, 1965, and some of the sidings have been lifted. *John Spencer Gilks*

Right: The Warwickshire Railway Society's 'Farewell to Steam on the LSWR' rail tour from Birmingham included Swanage on Sunday, 11 June, 1967. Rebuilt West Country class Bulleid Pacific No. 34004 *Yeovil* sweeps down the 1 in 80 gradient between the Catseye A351 road bridge and Woodpecker Cutting, near Eldon's Siding, around 2.30pm. Standard Class '4' tank No. 80146 is on the rear of the rake of eleven Mark One and Mark Two coaches painted in the new British Rail blue and grey livery. *John R. Coleman*

Below: No. 34004 *Yeovil* coasts into Swanage at 2.56pm with the 'Farewell to Steam on the LSWR' rail tour. Swanage signal box closed six days before on Tuesday, 6 June, 1967, and all signals have been stripped of their arms with the points locked. After 14 minutes in Swanage, the special train left at 3.10pm – with Standard Class '4' tank No. 80146 leading – bound for Dorchester and Weymouth. *Chris Phillips*

Above: The last British Rail steam train from Swanage to Wareham departs from Corfe Castle just after 2.50pm on Sunday, 18 June, 1967. With Standard class '4' tank No. 80146 at the front – and rebuilt Battle of Britain class Bulleid Pacific No. 34089 *602 Squadron* on the rear – the Railway Correspondence and Travel Society's 12-coach 'Farewell to Southern Steam Tour' has just crossed the stone viaduct and is heading up the 1 in 120 gradient towards Norden bound for Wareham and London. *Alan Trickett*

Above: The last British Rail steam train to Swanage at the stopblocks in front of the Railway Hotel after arriving at 2.26pm on Sunday, 18 June, 1967. Rebuilt Battle of Britain class Bulleid Pacific No. 34089 *602 Squadron* hauled the Railway Correspondence and Travel Society's 'Farewell to Southern Steam Tour' from London. With Standard Class '4' 2-6-4 tank No. 80146 on the Wareham end, the 12-coach train departed Swanage at 2.41pm. The public bar of the Railway Hotel was a favourite with train crews.
Andrew P.M. Wright Collection

Right: The historic train passes the site of the future Swanage Railway Norden park and ride station on Sunday, 18 June, 1967, on its return to Wareham. The long train headed by Standard Class '4' Tank No. 80146 is passing under the skew-arch bridge which carried the Pike Brothers Fayle and Company narrow gauge tramway linking the ball clay mines at Norden with the lorry loading point behind the photographer.
Michael Hardy

A final goodbye to steam. The photographer, who caught the previous picture, turned around to capture the last steam train from Swanage to Wareham passing the ball clay lorry loading point at Norden with rebuilt Battle of Britain class Bulleid Pacific No. 34089 *602 Squadron* taking up the rear. To the right is the rail-road transfer shed where ball clay in narrow gauge tipper trucks was dropped into lorries for export by road from the early 1960s until the end of 1970.
Michael Hardy

Final Diesel Years

Above: The start of a new era in the dying years of the Swanage branch, the first Bournemouth electrification 'push-pull' fitted Class 33 diesel-electric and 4TC carriage sets ran to Corfe Castle and Swanage on Saturday, 15 July, 1967. Making history, D6532 arrives at the terminus station with two 4TCs at 2.30pm with the 11.57am train from London Waterloo mistakenly displaying the Lymington branch '97' route code. Between 1967 and 1969, some London to Swanage trains were hauled by Class 73 and 74 electro-diesels. British Rail axed through trains in 1969 with the last Swanage departure for London on Friday, 3 October seeing Class 33 No. D6531 haul 4TC set No. 427. *Chris Phillips*

Left: Bournemouth driver Bill Henstridge in the cab of a non-'push-pull' fitted Class 33 diesel-electric on an inter-regional train at Swanage in the summer of 1967. Bill is wearing the new green diesel link uniform introduced by British Rail's Southern Region on Monday, 10 July, 1967, with the implementation of the Bournemouth electrification scheme and the end of steam traction. In the background is the abandoned goods yard. On the other end of the eight coach train was Class 47 diesel-electric No. D1922 as there were no run-round facilities at Swanage with the closure of the signal box in June, 1967. Bill was nicknamed 'Barney Rubble' after the character in the hit 1960s American cartoon series 'The Flintstones'. *Chris Phillips*

Above: It was ironic that 'Hampshire' and 'Berkshire' DEMUs ran on a dying Dorset branch line between 1966 and 1972. Built at Eastleigh in 1962, 'Berkshire' DEMU No. 1128 departs Corfe Castle with the 3.10pm train from Swanage on Thursday, 7 August, 1969. From October, 1969, British Rail timetables warned passengers the branch service could be withdrawn. With buck-eye couplings and Westinghouse automatic air and electro-pneumatic brakes, the DEMUs used six gallons of diesel fuel on each trip between Wareham and Swanage. *John Scrace*

Right: Three weeks before closure, 24-year-old Corfe Castle signalman Bob Richards takes the Worgret Junction key-token in its hooped pouch from Jim Evans in 'Hampshire' DEMU No. 1125 before giving the Bournemouth driver the staff for Swanage on Thursday, 9 December, 1971. No. 1125 was the first 'Hampshire' DEMU to visit the branch on Monday, 22 August, 1966, when used for driver familiarisation two weeks before the line was dieselised. At the rear of the train, village postman Rupert Blick unloads mail bags. Rupert's brother, Arthur, was a Worgret Junction signalman. *John A.M. Vaughan courtesy of Rail Photoprints*

Above: A depressing scene at Swanage in September, 1971, as three-coach 'Hampshire' DEMU No. 1124 coasts past the Victorian engine shed built in 1884 and abandoned by British Railways on the night of Sunday 4 September, 1966, when branch steam ended. The turntable – together with all signalling and track, except for the main running line – was cut up for scrap in late 1967 and early 1968. British Rail attempted, and failed, to sell the station site east of the Northbrook Road bridge for development during the final years of the branch with the plan being to set up a small platform and shelter in the foreground.
John A.M. Vaughan courtesy of Rail Photoprints

Left: Viewed from the Victoria Avenue road bridge on the outskirts of Swanage, 4TC set No. 411 and another four coach 4TC set in the new BR blue and grey livery are propelled by Class 33 No. D6521 on the 12.47pm train to London on Saturday, 26 July, 1969 – arriving in the Capital at 3.20pm. This was the return working of the 9.55am from London which reached Swanage at 12.30pm. *Roger Aldous*

Above: The abandoned goods yard and cattle dock at Swanage on Thursday, 4 December, 1969, after the tracks were lifted in late 1967. A green Southern National 1955 Bristol LS5G bus waits for its next run on route No. 419 to Corfe Castle and Wareham. Station foreman Jack Cannons was made redundant in October, 1969, after a 40-year railway career – the last six at Swanage. *Mike Turner*

Right: Amid an air of decay – and with driver 'Johnny' Walker at the controls – 'Berkshire' three-coach DEMU No. 1132 runs into the 'up' platform at Corfe Castle with a train for Wareham in July, 1971. To the right is the 12-lever signal box created from an extended porters' lobby in 1956 – replacing the wooden 1885 signal box next to the 'down' waiting shelter demolished in 1956 because of rot and subsidence. Built in 1962, No. 1132 was withdrawn in 2004 and preserved. *R.C. Riley*

Left: Framed by the fixed 'down' distant signal for Corfe Castle, three-coach 'Berkshire' DEMU No. 1132 climbs the 1 in 80 gradient from the Scotland and Arne road bridge with a train for Wareham during the summer of 1971. The 1962-built unit is about to pass the covered Eldon ball clay transfer siding closed in March, 1966. The narrow gauge ball clay lines here were last used in October, 1970, with the rails being lifted and the siding shed demolished by the end of 1971. Involved in the fatal Cowden rail crash during 1994, No. 1132 was withdrawn in 2004 and preserved. *R.C. Riley*

Right: With both carriage sets still in their 1967 BR blue liveries, three-coach 3TC No. 303 leads a four-coach 4TC up the 1 in 76 gradient towards the Haycraft's Lane bridge at Harman's Cross with the 2.47pm Swanage to London train on Saturday, 26 July, 1969. Propelling is Class 33 diesel-electric No. 6520 withdrawn in 1989. The train pulled into the Capital at 5.20pm and was the return working of the 11.57am train from London which arrived in Swanage at 2.30pm. *Roger Aldous*

Left: Push-pull Class 33 diesel-electric No. 6536 propels its two 4TC carriage sets – No. 427 in the new blue and grey BR livery leading – up the 1 in 78 gradient between the River Frome and the Holme Lane bridge with the 07.57am train from London which pulled into Swanage at 10.32am on Saturday, 26 July, 1969. The return working was the 10.47am Swanage to London train. No. 6536 was withdrawn in May, 1993, and preserved. *Roger Aldous*

Long-time Worgret Junction signalman Eddie Brown watches as driver Stan Chinchen on 'Hampshire' DEMU No. 1103 throws the hoop, with the single line key token from Corfe Castle, on to the catcher before the evening train from Swanage runs on to the main line for the journey's final mile into Wareham. Behind the driver is the compartment containing the unit's 4SRKT Mark Two 1,000 brake horsepower diesel engine.
Anthony E. Trood

The last summer of through trains from London at Corfe Castle. Viewed from the station master's house, Class 33 diesel-electric No. D6538 pushes 4TC set No. 427 away from the 'down' platform with the 3.30pm London to Swanage train on Thursday, 7 August, 1969. Arriving in Swanage at 6.09pm, the return working was the 6.14pm to Bournemouth which arrived in the resort at 7pm. No. D6538 was withdrawn in April, 1993.
John Scrace

The brave photographer has a head for heights in this 'aerial' view of Worgret Junction taken from the top of the main line 'up' home signal one evening in April, 1969. Three-coach 'Hampshire' DEMU No. 1103 heads for Corfe Castle while in the distance, beyond the A352 road bridge, can be seen the rooftops of Wareham. Built at Eastleigh in 1957, No. 1103 was withdrawn in 1979.
Anthony E. Trood

After through trains ended on Friday, 3 October, 1969, 4TC carriage sets and push-pull Class 33 diesel-electrics still ran to Corfe Castle and Swanage on ramblers' specials. Here, 4TC sets No. 407 and No. 426, with Class 33 No. D6580 at the rear pause at Corfe Castle before continuing to Swanage on Sunday, 6 April, 1969. Most of the track in the weed-ridden goods yard, closed on Monday, 4 October, 1965, has been lifted.
Anthony E. Trood

Right: With less than a year to go before the Swanage branch's closure, three-coach 'Berkshire' DEMU No. 1133 comes to a stop at Wareham's 'up' north bay platform No. 4 with a train from Corfe Castle on Friday, 29 January, 1971. Close to retirement, long-time Wareham shunter Bert Sansom watches the arrival. Built at Eastleigh in 1962 with a larger guard's compartment than the earlier 1957 'Hampshire' DEMUs, No. 1133 was withdrawn in 2004 and preserved. *Dave Mant*

Above: Swanage branch sunset as shadows lengthen and the line has just a few days to live. Three-coach 'Berkshire' DEMU No. 1128 arrives at Wareham's north bay platform No. 4 with a train from Corfe Castle and Swanage on the cold afternoon of Tuesday, 28 December, 1971. The same DEMU worked the branch for a week and three Bournemouth drivers were rostered during the day – a 4am early, 10am middle and 4pm late turn with crew changes at Wareham. *Alan Wild*

Above right: The last 4TC 'push-pull' carriage set visits Swanage on Saturday, 18 September, 1971, with the Poole Grammar School Railway Society's 'Dorset Venturer' rail tour. Push-pull Class 33 diesel-electric No. D6528 idles with 4TC set No. 403 during its five minute stop. Reaching the terminus at 1.39pm and departing at 1.44pm, the train carried passengers to Corfe Castle and Swanage after they missed their Wareham connection because of a late main line train. The special train was driven by Rodney White of Eastleigh and the guard was Ronald Spence of Weymouth. Withdrawn in 1991, No. 33 111 is preserved on the Swanage Railway. *John A.M. Vaughan/Andrew P.M. Wright Collection*

WITHDRAWAL OF RAILWAY PASSENGER SERVICE BETWEEN WAREHAM AND SWANAGE

The Southern Region of British Railways hereby give notice that on and from Monday 3 January 1972 the railway passenger service between Wareham and Swanage will be withdrawn and Corfe Castle and Swanage stations closed.

Details of the alternative bus services are available at local railway stations and bus offices.

≠ British Rail | Southern

Last Day of Trains

Left: In November, 1971, British Rail announced the closure of the Swanage branch would be on Monday, 3 January, 1972, with posters going up at Corfe Castle and Swanage as well as stations from Wareham to Bournemouth. Because there had been no winter Sunday branch trains since late 1967, the last passenger trains would ran on Saturday, 1 January, 1972 – New Year's Day. *Anthony E. Trood*

Top: Thee-coach 'Hampshire' DEMU No. 1110 in the 'down' south bay platform No. 1 at Wareham on New Year's Day, 1972 – the final day of passenger trains to Corfe Castle and Swanage. To the left is the water tower demolished in November, 1972. Built in 1957, No. 1110 was withdrawn in 1987. *Barry Thirlwall*

Left: Working on the Swanage branch's last early turn, driver Fred Norman observes the 10 mph speed limit as three-coach 'Hampshire' DEMU No. 1110 sweeps off the main line at Worgret Junction with the 12.41pm from Wareham to Swanage. In the cab, the second man is picking up the hoop and pouch containing the single line key token to Corfe Castle from relief signalman Walter 'Chalkie' White. *Barry Thirlwall*

Three-coach 'Hampshire' DEMU No. 1110 runs into Corfe Castle from Wareham past the decaying remains of the wooden 'down' platform waiting shelter. To the left is the station master's house where Jack Cannons, station foreman at Swanage from 1962 to 1969, lived with his wife. The last station master Bill Smith had moved on to Broadstone by the end of 1965. The Swanage branch closure made one 'Hampshire' DEMU redundant at Eastleigh depot and, as a result, unit No. 1110 was worked empty stock from Eastleigh to Tunbridge Wells West in Kent on Sunday, 2 January, 1972, for service on the Oxted to Uckfield line. *Les Tindall*

Signalman Arthur Galton takes the Worgret Junction key token from three-coach 'Hampshire' DEMU No. 1110 driver Fred Norman and gives him the staff for Swanage. To the left is the disused goods shed. After Swanage signal box closed on Tuesday, 6 June, 1967, the five-mile line beyond Corfe Castle was operated as an unsignalled long siding under 'one train' regulations with a staff. Formed in 1959, No. 1110 was withdrawn in October, 1987. *Les Tindall*

Above: Early and late duty Corfe Castle signalmen Arthur Galton and Bob Richards together in the box for the last time. Bob took his last trip on the branch before signing on for duty at 1.45pm while Arthur took his last ride after signing off from a shift that started at 5.45am. A Swanage and Corfe Castle signalman since the mid-1950s, Arthur was made redundant by British Rail while Bob started as a signalman at Wareham on Monday, 3 January, 1972 – the day the Swanage branch closed. Bob retired from Wareham signal box in 2007. *Peter R. Frost*

Top right: The last time the throaty growl of a 'Hampshire' DEMU would echo through the trees of the Wilderness, between the Pondarosa and Quarr Farm crossings, as No. 1110 – with driver Fred Norman at the controls – climbs the 1 in 76 gradient towards Harman's Cross with a train from Swanage to Corfe Castle and Wareham. Other Bournemouth drivers that worked the branch between 1966 and 1972 were Bill Henstridge, Jack Gardiner, 'Johnny' Walker, Fred Holloway, Eddie Thomas, Frank Riggs, 'George' Mansbridge, Reg Goddard, Percy Berrett, Den Scott, Stan Chinchen, Jack Hookey, Peter Grimes, Eric Croucher, John Rolls, Roy Adams, Peter Guy, Reg Mansfield. Dixie Dean and Bill Simons. *Les Tindall*

Left: Three-coach DEMU No. 1110 waits to depart Swanage for Corfe Castle and Wareham on Saturday, 1 January, 1972, while a yellow British Rail parcels lorry is parked next to the empty station master's house. The former goods yard is used for car and coach parking while behind the train is the Railway Hotel. The run-round loop was lifted in late 1967. *John R. Coleman*

An early 1960s Eastern Coach Works-bodied Bristol MW Western National No. 420 bus for Corfe Castle waits at Swanage while 'Hampshire' DEMU No. 1110 idles under the canopy before its next departure for Wareham. The journey to Wareham took 20 minutes for the train and 36 minutes for the bus. In front of the station is the Victorian Benn & Cronin information board for train departures and arrivals. The board was sadly broken up in July, 1974. *Dave Mant*

The last train prepares to depart Swanage with branch driver 'Johnny' Walker in the cab of three-coach 'Hampshire' DEMU No. 1110. Fellow 'Hampshire' DEMU No. 1124 was coupled to No. 1110 for the final train carrying 500 passengers issued with commemorative tickets – 50 pence for adults and 25 pence for children. Given the 'right away' at 10.15pm by long-time Swanage porter Bill 'Taffy' Hazell, the special train, nick-named by some of its passengers as the 'Purbeck Flyer', departed to the loud bangs of track detonators – placed on the rails by Bill – and ran into Corfe Castle at 10.24pm before arriving in Wareham at 10.40pm. *Ken Moore*

The End of the Line

The rusting tracks of the closed Swanage branch at Corfe Castle during June, 1972 – when Marc Bolan's T-Rex pop group was in the charts – just weeks before track lifting work by scrap merchants Eagre & Company of Scunthorpe symbolically started here on Monday, 10 July, 1972, in front of British Rail officials. The demolition operation then moved to Swanage. Ironically, that first day of track lifting at Corfe Castle saw the fledgling Swanage Railway Society hold an evening public meeting at the Central Collegiete Building in Gordon Street, London W.C.1., to discuss the rescue and preservation of the Wareham to Swanage branch line. *Gerry Andrews*

The final train ran to Swanage on Friday, 23 June, 1972. Hauled by Class 33 diesel-electric No. D6580, the works train picked up four concrete lineside huts from Swanage, Herston, New Barn and Corfe Castle with Southern Region travelling steam crane No. D.S. 414. The huts were taken to the Brockenhurst permanent way depot for main line re-use. D6580 was withdrawn in 1989. *Tony Trood*

The Townsend farmer's crossing bridge at Corfe Castle with the fixed 'up' distant signal stripped of its semaphore arm looking from the Swanage direction during the early spring of 1972 – three months after the last passenger train had run and four months before the scrapmen moved in to lift the track. The trackbed through here would be purchased from British Rail by Dorset County Council in March, 1974, for a village bypass that was never built. *Geoff Truscott*

By the second week of August, 1972, British Rail's demolition contractors – Eagre & Company of Scunthorpe – had lifted the passing loop at Corfe Castle. A crane loads rails from the lifted passing loop on to a flat wagon before being taken away by a Class 33 diesel-electric locomotive; the last train to run to Corfe Castle. British Rail would only sell the six and a half miles of land and track from east of Furzebrook to the Swanage Railway Society for £125,000 – a price the preservationists claimed was unaffordable and extortionate as they believed the worn track was worth less than £50,000. *Bob Richards*

Above: Viewed from under the 'up' platform canopy at Corfe Castle on an early morning in August, 1972, a Class 33 diesel propels its wagons along the 'down' line to where the scrapmen of Eagre & Company of Scunthorpe are collecting materials from the lifted 'up' passing loop. *Geoff Truscott*

Left: Looking towards Swanage, the Class 33 propels its train along the 'down' line at Corfe Castle to the starting signal prior to the scrapmen loading lifted track chairs up into the wagons. The lifting of the passing loop was the only occasion that materials were taken away by rail rather than road. *Geoff Truscott*

So hard to build, so easy to destroy. A depressing summer evening at Corfe Castle in August, 1972, and the Eagre & Company scrapmen have gone to the pub. By this time, the five miles of track from Corfe Castle to Swanage had been lifted using a mechanical excavator and taken away on articulated flatbed lorries supplied by British Road Services. The heavier concrete sleepers between Swanage and Harman's Cross had to be lifted by a large tracked road crane before being taken to Wareham and piled high on the site of the 1847 station master's house, opposite the signal box. Found to be unsuitable for main line re-use, British Rail sold the concrete sleepers to the Severn Valley Railway in March, 1978. Compare this same view in 1963 on page 43. *Bob Richards*

As David Bowie's 'Ziggy Stardust' song raced up the pop charts during the summer of 1972, the scrapmen were dismantling around a mile of track a week. At Corfe Castle in August, 1972, the 'up' line has been lifted – with track chairs thrown up on to the platform and rails awaiting collection. The 'down' line's wooden sleepers await digging out by mechanical excavator before being loaded on to lorries. *Bob Richards*

Lifted rails from the passing loop at Corfe Castle stored on a flat wagon wait to be collected from the headshunt at Furzebrook one lunchtime during August, 1972, as a Class 33 diesel-electric departs for Wareham with a rake loaded ball clay wagons bound for Poole, Eastleigh and ultimately the midlands' potteries. After the closure of the Swanage branch, the line from Worgret Junction to the Furzebrook ball clay siding was worked as a goods line under 'Regulations for One Train Working on Single Lines'. From Monday, 3 January, 1972, Furzebrook was served Mondays to Fridays by the 12.10pm Wareham to Furzebrook siding freight which returned to Wareham at 1.05pm. *Gerry Andrews*

The one remaining section of track at Swanage waits to be lifted in this view from under the Northbrook Road bridge lookng towards the goods shed and platform. A Southern National bus sits in the goods yard before its next trip to Corfe Castle and Wareham while the Second World War air raid shelter and former weighbridge building disappear among the weeds. *Geoff Truscott*

It is July, 1972, and tracklifting at Swanage is in its first week or two – rails and track chairs have been removed while wooden sleepers wait to be dug up by mechanical excavator. Viewed from the Northbrook Road bridge, tourist coaches and a Southern National bus park in the former goods yard. Swanage Urban District Council bought the station from British Rail in March, 1974, amid plans for a hotel, pub and car park on the station site. *Gerry Andrews*

By the end of August, 1972, all that remained to be collected from the trackbed at Swanage were the 45 feet rails and fishplates – the wooden sleeprs and cast iron chairs having been taken away by lorries in this view showing the engine shed and Northbrook Road bridge taken from the Swan Brook stream bridge. Many of the wooden sleepers were purchased by local dealer Brian Hallett of Ridge, near Wareham, who sold them to the fledgling Swanage Railway in the late 1970s. *Geoff Truscott*

Looking towards Herston, a few sleepers await collection by lorry from the old coaling stage at Swanage in late August, 1972. After the line was lifted, there was a suggestion for an access road along the trackbed from a demolished Victoria Avenue road bridge to a proposed new supermarket and car park built on the station site but the development never took place. *Geoff Truscott*

A sad scene at Corfe Castle one summer evening in August, 1972. Most of the track has been lifted – with sleepers awaiting collection by lorry – is this view taken by one of the station's former booking clerks and signalmen who started at Corfe Castle as a trainee porter in 1962, ten years later witnessing the closure and demolition of his branch line. Until the late 1980s, the railway trackbed was one of four proposed routes for a long-awaited village bypass. *Bob Richards*

Rail has the last laugh over road. A British Road Services articulated flatbed AEC Mercury lorry carrying lifted track chairs has become stuck in the ballast at Swanage; a situation that frequently happened during the lifting of six and a half miles of track during July and August, 1972. The fledgling Swanage Railway's first scraps of track were laid here in 1977 by volunteers – many of them teenagers. *Tim Deacon*

The end of the line. Half a mile east of Furzebrook, at Motala, where track lifting stopped at the end of August, 1972, and British Rail set up a stopblock. Few people thought the branch line to Corfe Castle and Swanage would return but the Swanage Railway's relaid tracks reached here on Thursday, 3 January, 2002 – the 30th anniversary, to the day, of the Swanage branch's official and controversial closure. Having taken just seven weeks to lift the tracks for scrap, it took dedicated volunteers 30 years to relay them – proving that preservation really is the art of achieving the impossible! *Gerry Andrews*

Gerry Andrews captured these evocative photographs of the abandoned Swanage branch during the winter of 1972 when everyone thought it was the end ... but it was just the beginning!

Above: The sun sets on an abandoned and desolate Corfe Castle station where there is nothing left but memories.

Below left: The trackbed already starts to flood past the former Eldon's Siding, north of Corfe Castle.

Below right: At the A351 Catseye bridge – between Norden and Motala – the ruts from the scrap merchant's tractor and flatbed lorries are still clearly seen in the granite ballast.